# The JOY of HIGH PLACES

PATTI MILLER is the author of nine books, including best-selling memoir-writing texts and the award-winning narrative non-fiction book *The Mind of a Thief*. She has published numerous articles and essays in national newspapers and magazines. She grew up on Wiradjuri land and now lives in Woolloomooloo on Gadigal land. She teaches memoir workshops around Australia and in Paris and London.

*To the bird-children*

# The JOY of HIGH PLACES

Patti Miller

NEWSOUTH

'A moving meditation on the way we doggedly court both bliss and death. Though Patti Miller strides the world in her hiking boots, and though her mind ranges through world history, mythology and societies, this danger-defying philosopher remains unmistakably, quintessentially Australian.'

Sue Woolfe, author of *Leaning Towards Infinity*

---

'A clear-eyed celebration of the capacity for joy and risk that makes us human. I finished this book feeling quietly elated.'

Delia Falconer, author of *Sydney* and *The Service of Clouds*

---

'A true tale of daring and endurance, pain and exuberance, told like a myth, *The Joy of High Places* is the most transcendental, most spiritual book written by a non-believer I've ever read. Strange, compelling, irresistible – it sings with poetry and wisdom, and keeps surprising to the very end. Creative non-fiction at its finest.'

Lee Kofman, author of *Imperfect*

---

'Each time I opened this book, I felt as though I was returning to a wise and true friend. Patti Miller captures the pleasures of the body, the joy of landscape, the thrill of knowing and being known. More than that, she unpacks the mysteries of memory, and the way we carry our past into our present. I loved it.'

Kathryn Heyman, author of *Storm and Grace*

'Patti Miller is a national treasure, who has not only led the way in gently parsing the past – both personal and collective – in her previous books, but has guided many of us on our own writing journeys. This new book is a delight to read, filled as it is with the "soul oval" of "wild joy" that she describes from childhood, a feeling she re-experiences in fleeting moments on her long, questing walking pilgrimages. It's also a moving portrait of a once-strained sibling relationship: a sister bound to the earth; a brother drawn to the sky. In the face of trauma, Miller writes this book to heal old wounds, to truly get to know her brother, and in doing so, she discovers a shared sibling language of joy (in walking, in flying) – as well as awe for all that remains mysterious in a loved one who is on the other side of tragedy.'

Ceridwen Dovey, author of *In the Garden of the Fugitives*

---

'A superb, soaring memoir of longing, resilience and delight in the natural world. Patti takes us with her through some of the most beautiful parts of Europe, describing the simple pleasure of walking and how it has held her captive throughout her life. Alongside is the story of Patti's brother finding transcendence in flight, the agony of it being taken away and the determination of mind over body.'

Jemma Birrell, Creative Director of Tablo Publishing

A NewSouth book

*Published by*
NewSouth Publishing
University of New South Wales Press Ltd
University of New South Wales
Sydney NSW 2052
AUSTRALIA
newsouthpublishing.com

© Patti Miller 2019
First published 2019

10 9 8 7 6 5 4 3 2 1

This book is copyright. Apart from any fair dealing for the purpose of private study, research, criticism or review, as permitted under the *Copyright Act*, no part of this book may be reproduced by any process without written permission. Inquiries should be addressed to the publisher.

ISBN:  9781742236513 (paperback)
       9781742244587 (ebook)
       9781742249070 (ePDF)

 A catalogue record for this book is available from the National Library of Australia

*Design* Josephine Pajor-Markus
*Cover design* Peter Long with Josephine Pajor-Markus
*Cover image* Peter Long

All reasonable efforts were taken to obtain permission to use copyright material reproduced in this book, but in some cases copyright could not be traced. The author welcomes information in this regard.

# Contents

The man who fell to earth  *1*
Childhood dreams  *6*
How the story came to be told  *15*
What are you doing out here?  *24*
Gods and monks  *52*
Icarus  *59*
Chronologies  *78*
A handful of people  *84*
Lucy  *99*
Walking around the mountain  *112*
Lazarus  *129*
The Fates  *141*
The Uluru offering  *145*
Phoenix  *159*
The Rosetta Stone  *169*
Phoenix rises  *189*
Becoming wild  *195*
A short walk home  *218*
Chrysalis  *227*
Acknowledgments  *237*

# The man who fell to earth

One day a few years ago, one of my brothers fell to earth and smashed his spine in several places when his paragliding wing collapsed. He believed he was going to die and then, when he realised he was still alive, he thought he would never walk again.

That's the most straightforward way to begin the story, but, of course, it's not necessarily the beginning. Many things happened before that; the dreams Barney had as a little boy for one, flying over the farm where we all grew up, swooping above the paddocks and fences in the night; that could be the real origin of everything that happened to my sensible brother. Or it could be more scientific to start with the weather, the rain damping down the silent grass, the unstable air producing patchy bullets of up-current, the warm pocket of air under a cool layer spinning into the hidden dust devil that brought him down. Or perhaps the real story begins eons ago in his genes, the particular and peculiar combination of methodical good sense and the longing for transcendence that he inherited from his German and Celtic ancestors. How far back would that make the beginning?

And neither is the story all about him and his flying and falling. The year he fell out of the sky, I began long-distance walking, which, in a way, is as absurd a means of getting about as flying under a piece of nylon cloth – albeit a lot safer. It is a ridiculously slow method of traversing the countryside, not much happens for hours, feet become painful, you get too hot, you get caught in storms, dogs snarl threateningly. But it is democratic – anyone with two legs can walk, it requires no training, once you've bought solid walking boots it costs very little money, and doesn't usually risk anyone's life. Walking is fundamental, everyday, without drama.

Flying is faster and more graceful, but it depends almost entirely on what appears to be the random and therefore unpredictable movement of invisible flows of air. It requires a high degree of skill and strength, it's dangerous, it's otherworldly. Imaginary beings fly – angels, dragons, fairies, griffins all soar with feathery or scaly wings above the earth in a detached parallel reality – while we who walk, un-winged, two-legged, are down in the folds of the earth with the sights and sounds and smells of the world right under our noses: a grub in a cocoon, the sweet clang of cowbells, sheep poo on the path.

On my two legs, I've walked thousands of kilometres across the countryside. I've walked day after day, week after week, for hundreds of kilometres on footpaths in France, England and Scotland, in Italy and Spain and Switzerland and in Australia, and most days I walk a quiet five kilometres to Mrs Macquarie's Chair on the sandstone headland opposite the Opera House near where I live in Sydney.

My brother has flown hundreds of kilometres over Bundjalung country in northern New South Wales and across the rainforests of southern Queensland, following where the *cloud-streets* let him fly. Other days he's flown only a few kilometres and realised that the air currents were not strong enough to take him anywhere and he's had to land again.

None of our journeys are continuous so there's not just one journey to follow from beginning to end for either of us. I can't draw one line for each of us and leave it at that. What is needed is a large paper map that I can fold out, smooth the creases and mark the walks and flights in different coloured pens. The journeys won't cross over geographically, that's clear already, but they are connected. For a start we are both making tracks, tracing visible muddy patterns on the earth and invisible airy arabesques above it.

In fact, I wonder if flying and walking are both a type of inscription on the world: footsteps in the dust, unseen patterns in the sky.

The reason I suspect walking, at least, is a kind of writing, is a slip of the tongue I've been making over the last few years. I've said walking when I meant writing, and writing when I meant walking, far too many times for it to be purely accidental. There's plenty of overlap. In both writing and walking you explore inner and outer landscapes: cliffs of fall, uneventful plains. And inner and outer weather: sunny, gloomy, stormy. There are hardships in both: getting lost, wondering which way to go, sometimes strenuous effort, sometimes ordinary plodding; and there are pangs of delight and even revelation: a valley in the Pyrénées afloat with white butterflies. In both, joy is rare and unpredictable, but it's worth it when it appears. In both, you hope to arrive somewhere, although at times you have to turn back to the beginning and start again. And most of all it's that each step, each word, connects you to the world, impresses you into it, makes you one with it. I imagine it's the same for Barney, that flying is a reflection of his inner life, but I don't know. The fact is, I don't know my own brother very well.

I have childhood memories of him; the two of us walking to the farm gate to catch the teacher's ute to school, Barney always a long way ahead; Barney saying, 'You have itchy-powder hair' – a mysterious insult unless you know 'itchy-powder' was our name for an ugly greenish sack that appeared at times in gum trees and which, for us, was a symbol of all that was revolting and disturbing. Of course I cried to our mother about that, and she said, 'Take no notice,' but I was a child and I did take notice. Years later, I believed Barney had forgotten all about it – the one who delivers childhood insults rarely remembers them – but when my first book came out, our mother said, 'Barney asked me what you had written about him. He must have a guilty conscience!' She had a wry expression on her face so I knew she remembered. I laughed – I hadn't said anything at all about him – but I was pleased in a childish part of myself.

Randomly distributed genes bring odd collections of people together. The vectors of lives intersect in families through shared inheritance and upbringing and then ricochet off into the future. When there's so many – there were eleven living in our battered old farmhouse – there's always going to be some missed connections, but for as long as I can remember, Barney, the third eldest of eight, held himself separate from the general melee of brothers and sisters, parents and grandmother. He had to share the boys' sleep-out with all the rest, but he kept his small area impeccably neat, as if there were an invisible wall beyond which the tide of shoes and dirty clothes could not flow. He had a box of comics stowed under his bed, which he wouldn't let anyone read – a distinct offence as everything (clothes, toys, books) was shared – and later he had a transistor radio which we were not allowed to listen to except on rare occasions of munificent bounty. He was tidy, methodical, rational, unemotional. It seemed that he disdained his family's general messiness – and my Irish red-haired temperament and disorderliness in particular. Decades later I was bewildered when he stepped off the side of a mountain into thin air as if he were a poet all along.

We inherited the same Irish, English and German genes – and some unofficial Wiradjuri and Asian – we were told the same God story of prayers and ritual, we walked on the same low rolling hills and plains. If you mapped our past, the lines would overlap for at least all the childhood years. Or perhaps not; perhaps we were always on different paths.

# Childhood dreams

I remember the Sunday that Barney stepped off one of the paths laid out for us. He simply refused to go to Mass. My father had gone into the boys' room to see why he wasn't ready. I followed him in.

'I'm not going,' Barney said. He had been sitting on the bed strumming his guitar, but he stood up when Dad entered.

To an outsider this rebellion might sound small, but such a refusal was unheard-of in our family – it felt as shocking as a declaration to commit murder. We weren't just Sunday believers; our every day was shaped around religion. We prayed the Rosary on our knees every night, recited more prayers before we went to bed, learned our catechism, examined our conscience and understood sin.

Dad was a gentle man by nature – Mum used to say he would walk away rather than have an argument – but rigid in his religious beliefs, and on the day Barney refused to come to Mass, he tried to force him. He grabbed him by the shoulder. Barney was 15 by then, dark-haired and skinny but taller than our father, and he pushed his hand away.

## Childhood dreams

'You're as bad as a Communist, making people do things they don't want to do,' he accused.

I stood there, terrified, knowing there was no worse insult to my father, who prayed every night for the downfall of Communism. And then our gentle Dad lifted his fist and punched Barney about the head and shoulders, several times. I can still feel the shock and the fear at seeing my father lose control of himself. I feel disloyal writing that, and, in fact, when I wrote this once before, I softened it to 'started pulling him', but memory stands firm against the written word. It was the most frightening thing I'd seen in my peaceful childhood, and it's the only time I can recall my father losing his temper with any of us. Still, he did lose it and he did attack Barney with his fists, which, I imagine, only hardened my brother's resolve against religion.

The side paths and deviations are hard to track in anyone's life. It's easier to think there's one path with a few twists and turns when, in fact, they are multiple, braided, for all of us. And every moment along every one of those braids contains another possibility, another way through the maze. I was going to say labyrinth, but there is only one way through a labyrinth, one entry and one central destination, so it was a key symbol for the Catholic church. Barney decided there was nothing at the centre and gave up on the labyrinth when he was a teenager. How he plotted his life after that, I don't really know. Maybe, like me, he made it up as he went along.

Our paths didn't cross over very often after we both left home, but there was one meeting I remember clearly. It was decades after our childhood on the farm, the immersed years that last forever. We had arranged to meet at the Fountain cafe on a shady square near where I live in Sydney. I hadn't seen him for a long time. He and his wife, Jenny, lived over eight hours drive away in northern NSW, and neither of us had been much inclined to breach our mutual incomprehension. We were both there, I suspect, out of family duty. I think he was actually visiting one of his daughters and added me into the arrangement. This was after he started flying, but before he fell.

I knew the man sitting in front of me, still skinny and dark-haired, was the boy who had inhabited the same dry landscape as I did, and had lived in the same falling-down house and who had defied our father one Sunday morning, but he seemed a stranger to me, had always seemed a stranger.

It was sunny that day at the cafe in Kings Cross. We were sitting outside under umbrellas, looking towards the dandelion spray of the El Alamein fountain. Anthony, my partner, was at the table, and Jenny, but I don't think their daughter had arrived yet. Virginal white seagulls and dirty ibis stalked around the fountain pool looking for scraps. Nothing about the place connected to our shared past, no context for a meeting of minds, but something did happen there. It was the first time I realised I may have got my brother completely wrong.

'What's it like?' I asked. 'Flying like a bird?' I hadn't seen him since he had taken it up a few years before. A polite question.

'It's the most extraordinary experience of my life,' he said.

I looked at him, startled. Barney was not given to hyperbole. His eyes lit up in his narrow face. He has our mother's dark Irish look, high cheekbones, wiry body. When he shaved his beard off – about the time everyone else was growing one – it was obvious he was identical to her adored brother, Jack, who had died in a car crash when we were children.

'Really?' I said. It was as much as I could manage. My tone wasn't doubting, just shocked.

'There's such a feeling of great power when I'm first surging upwards and swinging around like those swing-out horses on a merry-go-round. And on a smooth glide, it's peaceful and calm and I feel so joyful – I'm actually 4000 feet above the ground! Or higher. It's dreamlike to be sailing along in the sky, talking to a wedge-tailed eagle, looking at the world from above.'

My pragmatic brother chatting to wedge-tailed eagles? Talking about peace and calm and joy? I was rattled. And there was something else niggling. What was he doing being the poetic, untethered one.

'When I'm on a strong climb I feel totally exhilarated and when I'm well into a cross-country flight there's such a feeling of mastery – I'm actually a human flying! And I look down and see the beautiful highlands beneath me. The view from just under the clouds …'

His eyes and face were shining and I couldn't hide my astonishment. I didn't know who this enthusiastic, passionate brother was. He had become a winged creature, swooping and soaring with snowy-feathered wings in the heavens, communing with sky dwellers, looking down on the wide green earth below … He sounded like someone in love, or someone with a wild excessive temperament.

He saw my look and changed tack.

'I mean, it can get really cold high up and even with thick layers of clothes and gloves it can get so cold it's painful. And it can be a battle to keep the wing stable – it can become quite unruly and even collapse suddenly.'

It was too late. I'd already seen his wild bird soul and wasn't going to be fooled by the practical, taciturn mask he had perfected.

'Well, I hope that doesn't happen to you,' I said, a bit too shortly.

Later I rang Mary, my younger sister.

'What about Barney and flying!' I said. 'It's like he's someone else!'

'I know,' said my sister. 'Haven't you talked with him about flying before? Isn't it incredible!' She laughed with delight.

'I feel like I've only just met him – like, who is he?'

'I think he's only just met himself,' she said. We all knew Barney was the one on the outside. There was no antagonism, just that none of us knew who he was.

'I guess,' I said.

After the phone call I wondered why I felt put out.

In the decades when I hardly saw Barney, there were not even phone calls or letters. Whenever we did meet – a few dutiful family visits by me, then once for Dad's funeral, and once to help paint Mum's house – there was civil, but not open, conversation. It was hard to imagine we had grown up on the same farm, in the same family.

Our judgments of each other had developed. I talked too much, theorised too much, was too fanciful, too messy; he was too technical, too orderly, too detached, and didn't seem to need any communication with the world other than with Jenny. He looked after his children, provided them with flute lessons and took them to basketball matches and drama classes on his primary school teacher's pay, but didn't appear to know how to connect to them. He had an almost eugenic disdain for lack of intelligence, and for those who couldn't manage their lives. When we visited, there were topics we hopped around. I thought of him as clever and practical – and someone who didn't have a lot of heart, nor poetry in his soul. Maybe I was wrong about both.

Back at the Fountain cafe, I tried to rearrange decades of judgment. Barney talked about the practicalities of flying: the facts of the weather, especially the wind, of launching safely, of being able to control his 'big sheet of plastic'. I relaxed. This is what I expected of him, not spiritual joy and oneness with the elements and with eagles. Not Barney.

He started with the equipment. A paraglider, he explained, unlike a hang-glider, has no frame, relying only on air currents and the skill and sensitivity of the flyer to stay aloft. A hang-glider remains wing-shaped whatever you do, but a paraglider needs to be readjusted every moment. It requires a much more intimate relationship with the wing. His first paraglider was a second-hand Swing Arcus 3, red on top, white underneath. His current glider was an Alpina 2, red, orange and green on top and again white underneath. Its new shark-nose profile was solid at accelerated speeds and was resistant to spin and stall and it weighed 800 grams less than the earlier model, he explained. The Ronstan pulleys made engaging the speed bar and maintaining pitch control a pleasure and the wing design had created a huge reduction in parasitic drag.

Then there were the instruments: a 3D GPS, altimeter, variometer, compass, thermal tracker, ground speed indicator, wind speed and direction indicator, and flight recorder. Plus a VHS radio and a SPOT tracker, which provides GPS tracking of his flight to a central site known as SPOT HQ and also directly to Jenny's phone. If he was in danger he could press SOS and SPOT would alert emergency services with his exact location.

I did try to listen to my brother's explanations but I find it hard to pay attention to this kind of technical information and my brain blurred. Still, I did understand the dedication to equipment.

With walking it begins with boots. On the first long walk over the Pyrénées I thought my street boots would do me fine. They were ordinary lace-up boots with a flat heel, worn-in comfortable, and I didn't want to buy specialised equipment to use once a year. It seemed an indulgence to have exactly the right thing for everything; it was better to make do with what I had. But I discovered you do need the right kind of walking boots. After getting home from the Pyrénées, I bought a pair of leather Scarpa boots, heavy and thick-soled – and their lovely weight pleased me as soon as I put them on. They are scuffed now and the thick tread is worn down from a few thousand kilometres of walking but whenever I pull them on, they transform me into an Amazon and I eat up the trail, spin the earth under my heel.

The next most important object is the backpack. It has to be light and built to carry the weight on hips rather than shoulders. The feeling I have for the pack is not as strong as the almost idol-worshipping attitude I have towards the boots, but it still feels like a dear companion.

And then there are the walking poles, third in in the trinity of venerated objects. They represent another whole level of dedication, or even obsession, transforming me into a stick insect or long-legged goat as I clamber four-legged down steep paths, or an automaton as I stalk across flat landscapes. They can be used to point out wind-carved rocks, bird nests, a horse-drawn caravan, and to threaten snarling dogs.

I honour the boots, pack and poles not just for their usefulness, but for coming with me; they are fellow adventurers. I have relied on them and I wouldn't abandon them, even after they are worn out. I noticed recently my younger son, who also walks long distances, has kept his original backpack in the back of his wardrobe even though it is ragged and can no longer be used. It makes me think that in the human soul there is a fellow feeling that extends to wood, silk, stone, steel, leather, even Gore-Tex.

Then there is the compass and map. I have an old double-sided brass compass with a lovely quivering needle and a glass cover, but it's not taken walking because it's heavy. I take a modern Scandinavian one instead, a flat plastic rectangle, which is light and threaded with a red cord so it can be carried around the neck for quick checks. Just having a compass is a talisman against losing your way.

The compass was, in fact, first used for divination, a metaphysical way-finder, when it was invented during the Han Dynasty in China, around 200 BC. It was before the Vikings discovered magnetite, the lodestone, as a way of knowing north, south, east and west; of literally finding your way. The Vikings also used a sunstone, a crystal of Icelandic spar or andalusite, which polarised light so that they knew where the sun was, even when it was obscured by fog. Now there are satellite navigation devices and no need of compasses or maps or sunstones, just a voice telling us where to turn next. But that's too pinned down, too exact. You need at least some possibility of getting lost. How else do you find something that you didn't know was there?

# How the story came to be told

It wasn't until Barney fell out of the sky and was told he wouldn't walk again that flying and walking started to float together in my mind. We had both been tracing tracks across the world – he in the sky, me on earth. Neither of us really understood why we'd been doing it. I kept notes about my own walking, brief jottings in small notebooks, but I didn't know anything about my brother's journeys.

I asked Barney would he mind if I asked him a few questions about flying. This was a while after his accident, and after all that he'd been through I thought he might not want things stirred up. I don't really get that – I'm all for stirring things up – but I accept it's not the same for everyone. But he said yes, he was happy to talk about it. We started exchanging emails and phone calls and an occasional meeting when either one of us travelled north or south. It felt strange at first.

'So why did you want to fly? When did you get the idea? What was it like the first time?' We were back at the Fountain cafe, mid-summer I think. I had seen him a couple of times in Byron Bay when I was working, but it seemed risky to ask such questions so close to where it had all happened.

'The moment my feet left the ground and I was lifted into the air on my first high glide, it was exactly how it felt in my flying dreams when I was a kid,' my brother said.

'What were your dreams like?' I'd had flying dreams as a child too.

He explained that he ran one or two steps and lifted off easily and flew upwards as if he were swimming up from the bottom of a pool, almost stroking through the air. He could see the farm from above, ploughed paddocks, the roof of the shearing shed, sheep and cows at the dam. In one dream he taught our older brother, Peter, and younger brother, Tim, to fly from the top of the woodheap. In another he was standing at the fence at Granny Miller's house in Wellington, our nearest town, talking with the kids next door, when he calmly lifted off and swooped about as he pleased. He said he sometimes lost confidence and fell towards the ground, but he always regained his self-belief just before he hit the ground and was able to soar upwards again.

'Not like life,' he said wryly.

'Are you okay?'

'Yeah. I'm good,' he said. He shifted in his chair. This was way before he began admitting to being in constant pain. Saying things out loud can undo you.

'Can I backtrack for a sec. Where was it, your first flight?'

'A place called Possum's Shoot, it's a launch site a few kilometres from the Byron Bay turn-off. It was only for about five minutes. I flew into some lift straight away and it took me up along a ridge.'

'So how was it like your dreams? The first time, I mean. Can you remember?'

## How the story came to be told

'I'll never forget it. The sensation was just the same as when I was a kid. Not the position or anything, the feeling. I can remember the feeling in the dreams and it was the same. I soared upwards, and I swooped and turned into the wind and hovered like a hawk. To move to the left I just leaned my body and off I flew. And then when I pulled my hands down, it was as if my wings were curving downwards and I slowed down like a bird landing. I had never felt anything as exhilarating. I couldn't stop smiling; my whole body wanted to laugh with joy.'

Again that feeling in me – what was it? Envy? Perhaps. But it was also like the awe and fear you feel in seeing a newborn. A being freshly revealed – you almost don't want to look because you know what can happen to anything unprotected.

And I felt left out. My flying dreams didn't make me yearn to fly. In my dreams, I had to run fast before I could take off and my flying position was upright with my legs tucked up, almost to a squat. I can still remember what fences looked like from a few metres up and the feel of cool, dark air on my face. I was convinced that it was real, not a dream, even though most of the flying was at night. Since talking to Barney, I've asked all my other brothers – Peter, Tim, Kevin and Terry – and both my sisters – Mary and Kathy – who have all told me that they flew in their dreams too. Some of us are sensible and practical, some of us dreamy, but somehow, all of us growing up on Wiradjuri land became bird-children in the night and our mother and father never even suspected.

But Barney had attempted to fly in waking life as a child as well. He built wooden wings, nailing boards together in a rectangle, like aeroplane wings rather than a bird's, which clearly didn't work. He made a parachute from a blanket and binder twine, which also didn't work. It didn't stop his Icarus yearnings or his Daedalus constructions. He made dozens of balsa wood model aeroplanes and paper kites, and designed and made one powered model aeroplane, which he never flew because he didn't have the money to buy fuel. After he mentioned them, I did recall the parachute and the balsa wood planes and the kites, but I had no idea of the longing behind them.

We didn't share a childhood after all. We were each in a series of our own moments that we stitched together to create our own story. Deep in the neural pathways, neurones fire in intricate patterns, then the hippocampus joins endless nanoseconds together, creating reality. If we sew neatly, edit judiciously, no-one will see the gaps, the shimmer of the void beneath. It will appear to be one whole story, to make sense.

It makes me inclined to simply trace the pieces, the walks and flights, one by one, onto a shared map to see what happens. They happened in different times, are not chronological, but they might form a shape that I'm not yet aware of. Perhaps they will remain distinct. Stories are unpredictable, like walking and flying. As you walk or fly you depend on the weather, on air currents, on the body, on other people. You cannot control all the elements, and if you could, perhaps they each would be robbed of their essence, of their random ability to dissolve what has been certain.

I've decided to start unfolding the map and look at our journeys. The map is made of paper in my mind – I like the paper ones better than slithery phone maps – I enjoy the careful unfolding and then the refolding that is never quite right, and I like that they bear all the scars of my travels, the rips and stains and unreadable smudges. Smooth it out on the table. It's

## How the story came to be told

unmarked for now, but it already has the shadows of memory on it, and the blanks of unrecorded and forgotten observation.

Before I walk I always pore over an actual map – it's always the first thing I acquire, months earlier than I need it. A map lets you see what is possible. You can mark where you have been before and then the place-names on it inspire the next direction. It's like a story spread out into all its possible parts, before the elements have been selected and arranged in order, before a path appears. Walking begins with images in the mind, a place on a map.

Walking comes first. By nature we can walk, flying comes from human invention, which makes it seems logical to start with walking rather than flying. I look at my notebooks and few photographs. The notebooks are battered and stained from being squashed into my backpack and then pulled out each evening in a bar or cafe or hostel. They are written in cheap biro and contain lists, arrows, directions, observations. It's a scrappy record, not more than a few images noted each day.

The first image is thousands of bluebells, green forest paths, empty moors, soft meadows, larks singing and wild wuthering crags littered over the low hills of Wiradjuri country in central western New South Wales, a bewildering illusory layering over the drought-stricken land of my childhood. While Barney was trying to make wings and jump off the veranda roof, I dreamed of meadows and streams, the landscape of my reading. Real life was inside books; the rosy atmosphere in those mostly English worlds was the air I breathed. I inhaled it so deeply that illusion became more sustaining for me than actuality.

Still, even then, as a child I walked. I had to walk to school at first. From the age of five, I walked each morning with my brothers and a sister to the farm gate a kilometre away. There we climbed onto the back of the teacher's ute and were driven a few kilometres to the one-room school-house. In the afternoon, we were dropped off at the farm gate and walked back through the paddocks to the house. The first year of walking there were two brothers, Barney and Tim, and the next year another brother, Kevin, then a sister, Mary. The older two, Kathy and Peter, were in high school, riding their bikes to the bus stop at the end of the lane, and the youngest, Terry, was still a baby at home. There was no solitary walking.

In the morning we dawdled out the house-gate, unclipped the house-paddock gate near the kurrajong tree, and walked up the rise between the sheep yards and the creek then through the wire gate and along the track through the wheat paddock. The track undulated along the fence line, sandy and smooth, although occasionally muddy. In winter, the wheat was frosty, the frost starting to melt on each blade, leaving millions of glittering diamonds of dew. In summer, it was ripe yellow, heavy-headed; or already harvested, dry and spiky. After harvest, sheep were let in to nibble any leftovers and to graze on the lucerne planted between the wheat, making their own tracks across the paddock, narrow trails which they trotted along, one after the other. Sometimes we followed the sheep trails because they made a clear pathway through spiky burrs, an easy zigzag along the side of the hill.

Morning walking was cold, unwilling, red-nosed; afternoon walking was warm, with flies, sweat, skinned knees. In the winter there were icy puddles to break; in summer Barney ran past brushing the colony of flies off my back to make them buzz around my face.

How the story came to be told

In high school I rode my bike up the lane to catch the bus on the main road instead of walking, but I still roamed across the farm and across fences into other farms on the weekends. I walked in the winter when everyone else was sitting around the fire – a romantic pride in being out in the cold and wind when everyone else was snug. I walked over stubbly paddocks, looking down in case there was an Aboriginal axe, or a kangaroo bone. I climbed over the boundary fence, and walked across the neighbour's farm, heading towards a hill scattered with trees and rocks and covered in kangaroo grass and paddymelons; it was too steep to plough so it had been left untouched. It could reveal something hidden in the rough grass.

The map of bluebells – that's the right name for it – was unfolded, not the symbolic map of memory, but an actual paper map on the table in my kitchen. I had booked my ticket and was going to the United Kingdom to walk. Lower Slaughter, Pucklechurch, Tolpuddle, Dunblane, Zennor. Days were lost in the romance of names. The bubble of childhood reading expanded around my head making me feel as if I were floating in an overcrowded room. An idealised, never existing Enid Blyton world fogged everything. No precise path emerged. I didn't want to decide where to walk because that would mean ruling everywhere else out. Not every inch of earth can be walked.

I talked about it with Anthony, who walks with me. When I am walking, he is often there, even when I don't mention him for long periods. We have acquired the art of being alone together, each in our own walk, so perhaps the singular pronoun is just as accurate. Before and after walking is another matter.

Then we are together, reading and planning the next path.

He listened to the confusion about the multiplying nature of the map, then added a few complications. What about the weather? How far each day? I became practical. Given that it was autumn, it would make more sense to start in the north and walk south at that time of year in that hemisphere. And it had to be finished by a certain date. I had a writing class to teach in Paris at the end of it. There wasn't enough time to walk from John O'Groats to Land's End, but a series of walks from Scotland to Cornwall looked possible. The facts started to make a neat little wall against the vastness.

I found a walking site online that described paths all over Britain. A list of day walks appeared: the Cairngorm Highlands in central Scotland, Hadrian's Wall, the Lakes district, the Yorkshire Dales, the coast of Cornwall, the Cotswolds, and finally, part of the Ridgeway, one of the oldest walking paths in the country. I printed them out and located them on the map, and felt the relief of making limits: it gathers in sprawling infinity and defines what is possible. The walks had been followed by others many times, tracks worn into the earth, at times metres deep. The Cairngorms were first, the Lairig Ghru loop. It's time to trace the first lines on the map, to start the first walking story.

It flows out of childhood, but this walk isn't the beginning of my story with Barney. Our stories don't follow from one another, they run alongside each other and at times bend and cross over. He is not in my story for long periods, and I am not in his – although I am there, watching and listening, as he recounts them. We are not in the same geography for most of the time, and the chronology is staggered, in different time frames and measured in different units, his in moments, mine in years.

## How the story came to be told

I don't know that connecting places or time is what matters in our stories; it's more to do with what we each found, Barney and I, on our separate journeys, me on the earth, him in the sky.

# What are you doing out here?

*Scotland and England*

At the loch where our first walk, the Lairig Ghru loop, began winding its way towards the pass into western Scotland, a dense mist had fallen. It wasn't far from the pub where we were staying, but the mist gave the loch a detached, otherworldly air. It enfolded and then silenced ordinary conversation. All thought, all language, muffled. It was still, not swirling, allowing a world made only of the path and a few dim metres of lake. There were two white rowboats tied to white buoys in the whitish water-air, a monochrome world reduced to essentials like a Japanese meditation garden. Apart from the line of rope from one of the boats to its buoy, delicate as a thread of black ink, nothing was distinct. Sky and water were one. It was the kind of beauty that makes the breath almost stop, slowed down to the breathing of stones, of water.

The sky and loch were the colour of the soul I had imagined I had as a child – a whitish slightly grey colour, insubstantial and dense at the same time and impossible to grasp. In my child-mind the soul also had a shape, a long oval, but the loch and sky were without shape. At the time, when I stood at the water, gazing, and again now as I write about it, part of me wanted to stop there forever, as if I had arrived at the right place. Here I am.

And then I kept walking. It's the way of the world, and besides, it was much too soon to stop. The path led away from the loch into Rothiemurchus Forest through native Caledonian pines, gnarled and spare, and birches and purple-berried juniper. Unlike the bare and often ugly understorey of pine forests in Australia, where very little undergrowth has adapted to survive under pines, here grasses, sedges, mosses, liverworts, lichens and heather covered the ground. Rocks and fallen branches, the 'bones of the forest', in a quiet carpet of mottled sea-green and lemon yellow. Lichen-covered mounds looked like ancient woodland graves, as if bodies had fallen in ages past and were being absorbed into the earth. Although the forest was open and light – a soft, grey light – the spongy flora created an undersea feeling, a cool greenish quietness. Wood sedge, rock hair, witch's hair, spotted black foot, golden pine lichen, little clouds, coral crest, tree lungwort, heather-rags, woolly hair moss; their names a chant of old cures and spells. I couldn't help thinking magic must have been enacted here.

The thrill of difference made my heart seem louder in the stillness. I kept exclaiming about the quietness until Anthony's lack of response made me hear my own voice rattling around the pines.

After an hour or so, the path turned upwards and into heathland with wiry grasses and heather at the end of flowering. The mist had lifted but was threading around the mountains rising in front away in the distance. My spirits lifted. Although I grew up on low flat country, gentle undulations that could hardly be called hills, high country stirs an excitement in me, the same kind of electrical thrill that storms create. Wide desert with only horizon and sky is also powerful, but in a different way, calm and wordless. It's as if there are different chambers in the soul that respond to different landscapes: childhood plains for comfort and reassurance, deserts for peace, mountains for wild exhilaration. I remembered fragments of a poem from long ago – a man who lived on the lowlands whose wife yearned for the mountains; I've forgotten the poet's name but remember the desire for a mountainous landscape that could not be assuaged by anything else.

Anthony and I didn't talk much, just a few words about the map and written directions. It looked as if a storm might be coming in behind a dark mountain to the south-west – we could be caught without shelter. I didn't know how to read this landscape, whether it was dangerous to be out on such a bare and rocky route in an electrical storm, but neither of us was inclined to turn back. Every time I looked up, the mountain changed as veils of mist lifted and fell, making it difficult to estimate how far away it was and how far we had walked, but ahead I could see the *lairig*, the pass, drawing me on. I took a photograph on my phone, the foreground brown heather, a rocky dry watercourse, and ahead the pass, grey clouds swirling. It looks like a nineteenth century painting, its murky grey-brownness speaking of wildness and longing. We would not walk right through the pass, just the 20-kilometre return to the loch, but I could feel the ancient pull of a pass, the desire to see what might lie on the other side.

Below in a gorge was Allt Druidh, which in Gaelic means 'Snake Stream', although *druidh*, confusingly, could also mean 'charmer'. We reached the level of the stream and walked along it for a while until the path turned at right angles up a dangerously steep slope, heading away from the pass. I found myself on all fours, afraid of slipping on such a steep incline, ungainly, no longer a biped. It felt somehow disgraceful not to be two-legged, even for a short while.

On the heathland above, there was an art gallery of lichens: pale green, blue, frilly white and purplish black on large rocks of pink granite. I tried to identify them, but there are more than 1700 species of lichen in the British Isles, many of which grow in Scotland because of the purer air, and lichenologists – that's what they are called – can study one rock for hours to make an identification. Lichens were used for dying cloth: the greys and browns of Harris tweed came from *crottle* lichens right up until 1997, and a much sought-after purple or red came from *cudbear* lichen. The speckled shades and mottled patches on the pink rocks reminded me of the paintings of Indigenous Australians, the subtle colours and the patterns creating a geography of stories, if only I could read them. It was a wild landscape where only rough, scratchy trees and plants grew – too cold, too wet, too windy for gentle flora. Like the deserts in Australia, and much of the dry sclerophyll bush, it was not welcoming, not suited to an easeful human life. 'The nurse and tutor of eccentric minds, the home of the weird,' said Henry Lawson of the Australian bush, but he could just as well have been writing of the Scottish Highlands.

The path reached the Chalamain Gap where it disappeared into a ravine under a huge fall of boulders. The whole ravine was blocked and the only way through was to clamber over the boulders for at least half a kilometre. It needed concentration and careful use of walking poles not to twist an ankle or fall into a crevice, so the going was very slow. I was nervous, well aware that a slip would mean the end of our walking. The guide notes described it as 'easy scrambling' but not having done it before, I found it difficult and dangerous. At the same time, the stretching long-limbed ape-like movement of reaching from boulder to boulder was oddly pleasing. It felt as if I were turning into some other kind of creature, a rockmonkey-woman, stretching out each leg, steadying a foot, balancing with both pole-arms, swinging across empty space.

Halfway across we met up with the only other walkers we had seen, three men in their twenties who asked us to take a photograph of them on a huge boulder. They were elated at being halfway, and in high spirits, playful creatures leaping from rock to rock rather than the stretching, testing animal I'd been.

'Where are you from?' they asked, the usual question when a differently-accented English is spoken. 'What are you doing out here on this tough walk in the Highlands?' It wasn't really a question to answer, just a kind of compliment, an acknowledgment that none of us really knew what brought us here but that it was irresistible. It wasn't something anyone ever mentioned in the years I've been walking, but it was always there, the almost embarrassing mystery of why we walked pointlessly across the countryside. We know where are going – we have maps, there are signposts – but why? What are we doing out here?

On maps and signposts in the Highlands there were geographical words I didn't know at all and words I knew from books but had wrongly imagined. *Lairig* is the Gaelic word for pass, *Brae* is not a stream but the slope of a hill; *allt* is a stream; *linn* is a pool;

*tobrach*, a spring; *strath*, a wide valley; *ben*, a mountain; *clach* means stony; *creag* is a cliff, rock or hill; *còinneach* is mossy.

The words became a connection to place as much as my boots on the ground, a spell-path to the heart of the wild country. The names let me hold what I saw in my mind, a kind of possession. A kind of power, perhaps. At any rate I felt powerless when I didn't know what something was called.

It was the same when I started emailing questions to Barney. The answers were prompt and thorough, but I often didn't know what the words meant. Half-joking, I said he would have to write me a dictionary for his new sky-world language. The very next day, pages of definitions arrived. I was impressed – and disconcerted – by the fact that he had taken me literally and by the amount of work he must have done to assemble the 'dictionary' for me in such a short time. Some of it was technical: *carabiners*, *pod-harness*, *variometer*, *anti-G chute*; some of it explained shorthand terms: *cus* for cumulus clouds, *cumnim* for cumulonimbus, *CX* for cross-country flight; and then there were poetic words like *ridge-soaring, cloud-street, cloud-suck, bomb-out, spiral dive*. I could see the phrases flowing across the sky, describing arcs and leaps and falls, opening up a world I had not seen before, or at least not from that angle. I skipped over the technical words, but had to go back to them later. The exact language, the terms, mattered. I read and re-read his dictionary of the Foreign Language of Flying, delighting in the word-map and the way it revealed Barney's mind and the mind of his tribe. This was their language. I pictured him and the other flyers sitting on the mountain side and watching the weather, waiting for the wind to change or the drizzle to clear and speaking their own language, safe and whole in their shared net of words.

I didn't know what *fell* meant either until I came to the Lake District, a landscape that had become the sacred well of the English soul, especially since Wordsworth lived and wrote here. It wasn't until I arrived there and started walking that I realised the sacred well was not really the lakes at all, but the *fells* above them. *Fell*, a high and bare landscape, from the Old Norse *fjall*. It's not a word used to name any geography in Australia and I'd only come across it in passing in English novels. From the ordinary associations – a fell deed, fall, the fallen – I imagined *fells* as doom-laden lowlands. So strong was this wrongly pictured image that even now when I have walked across the extraordinary stark beauty of these highland moors, my first reaction to *fell* is still as if to gloomy lowlands.

There are 14 lakes in the district, scattered among hills and craggy mountains; one of them, Scafell Pike, the highest peak in England – *pike* is a local word for a pointed hill. The cold Atlantic winds sweep 140 inches (3555 mm) of rain across the district each year, creating a damp geography of *becks* and *burns*, peat *bogs*, *cataracts* and *tarns* nestled in hollows high on the fells. The lakes are marked by pretty tourist villages, but the fells have been left to themselves, except for hardy walkers and a few sheep.

We had driven down from the Cairngorms to Hadrian's Wall where we had stayed the night and walked the next morning along the misty wall. We arrived in the Lakes District late afternoon and stayed in a small bed and breakfast with a badgers' den at the bottom of its fields. The first walk towards Easedale Tarn began near Dove Cottage, Wordsworth's house, which I didn't visit. I wasn't here to pay homage to a Romantic poet, but I was impressed by his extensive walking – estimated at a mind-boggling 175 000 miles (281 600 km) over his lifetime – and by the fact that his writing was born from this landscape.

Perhaps the one thing I know is how a landscape forms a person. For me it hasn't so much been culture or the drama of experience that has formed the core of identity, but land itself, Wiradjuri land. For Wordsworth it was this place, its streams and lakes and fells, which he mapped almost inch by inch, moment by moment, in his poetry. Hundreds of his verses, he said, were written at Easedale Tarn and alongside the beck that ran down from it.

The path climbed steeply out of the town towards Silver How – *how*, from the Old Norse *haugh*, meaning 'hill'. Even in late September, it was hot work climbing the slope of slithery stones under a bright blue sky and I soon stripped down to a singlet. I stopped every few metres for water and to regain my breath; there was no shade and nowhere to sit down without having to brace my feet against slipping. It felt more like the stony badlands in a cowboy film than the wild and misty romance Wordsworth's poetry had led me to imagine:

> While thick above the rill the branches close,
> In rocky basin its wild waves repose,
> Inverted shrubs, and moss of gloomy green,
> Cling from the rocks, with pale wood-weeds between …

We reached a cairn of stones the guidebook had described. The guide then went on to say, 'there are a number of paths to choose from and I would advise keeping to the one that maintains the highest ground. It does look a difficult task of navigation on the map but it really is a case of following your nose.'

## The JOY of HIGH PLACES

As might be expected, our inexperienced noses led along a sheep-track through thick yellowing grasses and heathers – bell heather, bilberry, crowberry, cow-berry, according to the guide – that ended after a couple of hours in bracken and gorse. We had a detailed topographic map, but the phone-compass was out of range, so, without knowing where any of the features were, nor even their general direction, our best efforts at reading the place failed. By backtracking for a while we could see the lake on the left, and, using it as a direction marker, eventually found the way down to its furthest end. We had wandered 15 kilometres in almost exactly the opposite direction from Easedale Tarn.

The next day we walked again towards the tarn, this time by a different route that led directly to it along one of Wordsworth's becks. We carried small backpacks, walking poles, water bottles, a thermos, and sandwiches made by the bed and breakfast owner. There were a few tourists out in the early morning town, all of whom nodded as we passed them, but by the time we headed away from the houses, there was no-one else. It was a pretty walk, first along a stone wall–lined lane, then steeply up along the stream and then past a cataract that fell into a pool,

> … and made a song
> Which, while I listened, seemed like the wild growth
> Or like some natural produce of the air …

Below were fields of dried-out grass and tangles of bracken and stone sheep pens, now empty and unused. It was a sunny day again, the world felt at ease. There were herbs – agrimony, alpine blue-sow-thistle, crocus, basil, thyme, harebell, heather – on either side of the path. When we arrived at the tarn the

## What are you doing out here?

sun was shining on the blue-grey water, giving it a sparkling air, nothing like the 'black and sullen' appearance Wordsworth remarked on, and not inducing the 'melancholy natural to such places' he wrote of. He had walked all over this countryside in every sort of weather and saw it on bright sunny days as well – some of his poems are full of light and air, but the pervasive feel is of the deep power of melancholy places and days. It sounds like romanticism and I don't trust romanticism any more – but I do trust someone who has walked every day in every weather.

The mists were swirling in when we set out for Derwentwater the following day. The walk began at the small village of Grange, headed up to Cat Bells, back and over Maiden Moor to High Spy, then down through slate quarries. On paper, it was a reasonably easy walk, a stroll along country lanes under oaks, birch, larch and pines, surrounded by Enid Blyton country with wooden fences, flocks of sheep and stone houses, all gentle under a still mist. Shortly, the path left the country lane and became a narrow steep track towards Cat Bells, a long promontory overlooking Derwentwater. At one point, where the track seemed to wander in several directions at once, we met two walkers coming in the other direction.

'Where are you from?' The usual question, and the usual surprised response to finding walkers from so far away on this fell.

'It's a bit tricky after High Spy,' one of them said.

Anthony pulled out the sketchy map, and both walkers looked at it briefly.

'Can't really see it on there, but as you are coming down,

just before it levels, you head off to the left. It's a bit marshy, but then you get to a stile and after a while you head down through the shale mines.'

We wished each other well and then Anthony and I continued upwards until we reached Cat Bells. There was still mist rising from the lake, grey and gloomy, and a cloudy turbulent sky. It wasn't exactly raining, but the air was wet and, although it was mid-morning, the light was dim. We sat down on the side of the rocky crag and drank tea from our thermos, feeling as if we were in a quiet English novel. One black-faced sheep sat alone on the side of the hill contemplating the Wordsworthian view.

I felt connected and calm. A connection to place usually depends on a layering of memories, associations that colour everything with significance and with triggers for joy in the reassurance of history, but walking creates connection on its own, without need for a past. My boot on the soil created an intimacy without seeming to need memory; the slow pace, the second-by-second passing of grasses, mosses, stones, bushes, created closeness, a sense of sharing the same small patch of earth.

As I walked back down the saddle from Cat Bells and then over Maiden Moor, the feeling of contentment swelled – I could feel it causing my rib cage to expand. I became minutely aware of my body: the air in my lungs, blood pumping, leg muscles stretching and contracting, head clear and straight on my spine; my body awareness like a child's – lithe and strong and unconscious of appearances. A light rain had started to fall on the rough heath and wiry grass, and the path was rocky – nothing pretty here – but I could feel the 'soul oval' of childhood stretching out and filling with wild joy. I wanted to yell, jump out of my body. The exhilaration of high places buzzed in me. It's a curious excitement laced with longing that must have some biological purpose; perhaps a reward for our ancestors climbing up out of the Great Rift Valley in Africa at the beginning of human time to encourage us to walk further across the world. At last there was knowledge of the landscape from above; how thrilling was the scope of our vision. I thought of Barney hovering and dipping far above the hills and paddocks, like a large and reasonable eagle.

'Aaaaaahhhh!' I whooped. 'Aaaaaaahhh.'

Anthony, who was 20 metres or so ahead, turned around, startled. I shrugged and looked around from the top of the world, seeing the expanse of fells and sky in all directions, and noticed storm clouds to the west. I caught up to Anthony and we looked at the dark smudge on the sky.

'Which way will it go?'

'No idea.'

We had no way of interpreting or predicting the weather in this isolated place, no means of reading the relationship between sky and land. High Spy, above us, was rocky and exposed. There was nowhere to shelter, not a rock or a bush above knee height. We were about halfway and, without knowing which way the weather would go, we decided we might as well keep going forward as go back. We continued upwards as the westward sky darkened and lightning started to flash. I counted until the thunder crashed. It was still a few kilometres away.

Just after we reached the cairn on top of High Spy, there was an ominous stillness then the wind whipped around the hilltop. The black cumulonimbus clouds were now overhead and the time between the lightning flashes and thunder was much less. Without build-up, a pelting rain began to fall. My heart started to thump. I didn't know what we should do, which way would take us to safety. I was afraid in an elemental way, afraid of the elements. We took a quick look at the map, which was instantly sodden, and then almost ran downhill towards Dalehead Tarn. I was wearing a raincoat and pulled the hood up, but the heavy, driving rain already dripped from the front of my hair and trickled in under the collar. I cast around for shelter, but there was nothing.

And where was the turn to the left into the marshes the walkers had mentioned? The directions gave an ordnance map grid reference for the turn, but the map was disintegrating in the rain – we had not thought of putting it in a plastic sleeve. Anthony saw a line of lower heath that could have been read as a path, so we headed through the boggy ground, jumping from tussock to tussock, sometimes sinking as far as our knees. We helped each other to squelch free and then sank again. We came to a fence and a stile and half-ran on until we came to steps leading down through abandoned slate mines. At last we were coming off the fell, away from the electrical storm.

The rain was still heavy and the loose slate covering the steep steps slipped every time we trod on it. It was bleak and severe and a ridiculously dangerous place to walk. I descended like an anxious long-limbed animal with my sticks balancing each precarious step, fearful of slipping even in my deep-gripped boots. There were mines all the way down on either side, but our directions noted, 'these should only be explored by those with suitable experience' and by now I was feeling humbled enough to take advice.

Near the bottom of the slope we lost the way completely. We had crossed Tongue Gill, a stream running steeply downhill, a number of times, but could not find any of the other landmarks.

## What are you doing out here?

I tried crouching under a spiky briar bush to look at our map, but it had turned into a ball of paper mush. Anthony's phone compass was working so he tried to work out the direction of Grange village. Eventually we saw a group of walkers heading northwards on a road a few kilometres to the east. We kept them in sight, veering towards them until we were following and, after another half hour, found ourselves back in Grange, sodden and cold. Without knowing how to read the sky or the landscape, nor carrying a decent map, it was only luck that brought us safely off the fells.

I have to admit none of this would have happened to Barney. If he had been out walking on the fells he would have been well equipped and properly informed. When you are lost or caught in the weather on the ground it's frightening, but, unless it's extreme conditions, not usually life-threatening. Whenever you fly, reading the sky is essential, a matter of life and death. It's obvious if you, an earthbound creature, are going to step off the earth, then you need to know if there will be anything to stop you from falling. The skyscape, however, is invisible; the towering columns of warm rising air, *thermals*, the sheer cliffs of falling cold air, the direction and speed of *wind highways*, the endlessly shifting complexity of sky topography, are all only able to be read by their effects.

From his front yard in Murwillumbah, on a good day when the line of sight was not interrupted by clouds on the range north of the town, Barney could see the sky above Beechmont and even Mt Tambourine launch sites and could gain some idea of what the wind was doing from the shape and drift of the clouds. The 'best-looking' skies for long flights are mostly blue with well-formed cumulus clouds regularly placed across the sky, marking the tops of thermals – if the line is long, stretching for many kilometres, it's called a *cloud-street*. The highway of thermals, plus the latent heat of evaporation released during condensation, gives greater lift just below and in clouds. Overcast skies are not bad, but thermals generally won't be strong near the ground, and high up, dangerous embedded cumulonimbus storm clouds can be difficult to spot.

Barney also checked weather bureau information, including specialised weather forecasts for paragliding, and data from the wind stations at the launch sites. For take-off, wind speeds under 20 km/h are safest. Wind speed for long-distance flights needs to be between 20 and 30 km/h, although if you are flying in several directions, then lighter winds, under 15 km/h, are easier for cross- and head-wind legs. If you approach a thermal from the downwind side, you have to fly through a greater expanse of sinking air – not so good – and if you have a tailwind, your speed will increase and carry you forward as you climb – much better. If, however, the wind is too strong, thermals will lean over to the point where you can't climb fast enough to avoid falling over the edge of them. It's as if a thermal is a constantly rising invisible skyscraper, and if you fly too fast, instead of rising with it, you will tumble off the lip of the invisible building.

The landscape below needs to be read as well. Stubble paddocks, sheltered gullies and furrowed paddocks are *thermal collectors* where air warms and gathers, and creek-lines, edges of forest and ridgelines are *thermal triggers*. If you spot a trigger downwind of a collector, there will almost certainly be a thermal in that location. Movement of dust and leaves on the ground, especially spinning movement, needs to be noted because it indicates a whirlwind, or dust devil, which can shoot the unsuspecting flyer suddenly upwards and cause the wing to collapse.

Before he stepped off the side of the mountain for the first time, and every time, Barney watched the trees, clouds, birds and butterflies. He looked for soaring birds like eagles, ibis and pelicans for signs of thermals, and also insectivorous birds like swallows and swifts that had been drawn into thermals as they chased their prey. He looked for butterflies being drawn up – butterflies are effective *thermal markers* during flying. If you see a butterfly thousands of feet up, then you know it's in a column of rising air which can carry you, human and butterfly, where you might never have imagined. He looked at the launch-site windsock and leaves, branches and grass to judge wind strength, direction and likely turbulence and he noted the air on his face and body – was it warm or cool, was it flowing smoothly or in short sharp slaps?

It seems to me that my brother was attentive to every element of his airy world, his senses recalibrated to notice details that only a sky creature needs, his neural pathways redrawn, as if he had become part-bird, with a firing avian brain.

Our evolutionary paths parted company with birds as far back as the reptiles, but I still like the idea of a bird-snake-man hidden deep in millions of dark brain cells. Perhaps the child brain floats down into those dark cells to a time when beings had bird and human mind all at once, knowing the feel of wind under wings and feet on the earth. Perhaps indigenous stories from around the world are right; we really are magpie-woman, eaglehawk-man, sparrow-man, crow-woman, swallow-child, all of us every day, and not just in childhood dreams. We are land creatures, feet padding along on the soil; we see insects, stones, fences, animals, all at our own level, but deep in the cerebellum, we know the world from above.

For Barney the view from above was addictive. I had felt the excitement of high places, but not the utter strangeness of experiencing height without anything beneath my feet. Later, when I sat down to write his stories I realised what I didn't know. The particular details matter. I emailed to ask him to tell me what it had been like lifting off and then up into that sky world and he wrote back that afternoon.

Each time he took off, grasses and rocks were close and distinct, his feet skimming just above them, his view rocking back and forth as if he were swinging on the end of a large pendulum as he stabilised his wing. Within a few seconds, the slope fell away and he was looking down on eucalypts, still close enough to see leaves and branches. Then when he caught a thermal early – on his first fight – he soared upwards, the earth seeming to fall, the horizon opening up so that he could see the whole landscape of the Eastern ranges inland from Byron Bay. From his *pod harness* – a kind of strap chair with his feet held out in front in a covered cocoon – he dangled under a red and white wing. He moved at 35 to 40 kilometres per hour and looked down on the world.

Below were eroded plateaus, ridges with steep-sided valleys – the ridges and valleys cleared, and the steeply sloping sides thickly wooded with patches of rainforest in the deeper valleys. When he looked down he could see brilliant green paddocks, miniature farm animals, sheep tracks, the dark smudge of eucalypt stands and forests, sandstone cliffs, creeks, gullies, cloud shadows, roads, mountains, undulating hills. When he looked ahead he could see blue sky, white and grey clouds, crows, eagles, hawks, and the horizon. Above the patterned world, he felt delight in the beauty of the landscape mixed with a kind of disbelieving astonishment that he was doing something so far outside the limits of what a human body ought to be able to do.

After I read his notes I wonder if the joy of walking might be the opposite; a return to the original capacity to stand upright and walk, two-legged, across the earth on the African savannah. Not a breakthrough to a new experience, but a return to an ancient one. In nature, not above it. When I asked Anthony where he thought the delight lay he said, 'It's primordial. Back to the beginning, what our bodies were built for.' I knew wasn't suggesting an Almighty plan, just that there is an inherent pleasure in a body working well. Our legs carry us up hills, across streams, over prickly moors, up rocky slopes; traversing the open country to the next human settlement. It's as if I walk with my ancestors when I walk across the landscape, all the way back to my first bipedal ancestor.

After walking in the Fells, we drove to Yorkshire. The speedy passing of the countryside made little impression, the feeling of it being an overview robbing it of any intimacy. Country needs time and stillness to do its work. A walking pace. And walking needs to be purposeless. It seems contradictory, walking should be meaningful because it has a purpose, that's how the world works – meaning is derived from purpose – but the opposite seems to be true. It's true that the aim is to get to your destination for that day, but it's how it unfolds that matters more than arriving. If it was just 'to get there', then I'd surely climb in a car.

# The JOY of HIGH PLACES

But once we reached the Yorkshire moors and dales I realised I did recognise them. Writing had done its work in the teenage girl walking on the farm, immersed in the wild landscape of Heathcliff and Cathy although there was nothing resembling it around her.

> I was only going to say that heaven did not seem to be my home; and I broke my heart with weeping to come back to earth; and the angels were so angry they flung me out into the middle of the heath on the top of Wuthering Heights; where I woke sobbing for joy.

I remember the deep sense of both disturbance and recognition those words caused in me. Even decades of ordinary life later, Cathy's words create a pang. Perhaps I was beginning to see, even then, that I also might prefer the actuality of earth to the idea of heaven. I belonged in the smell of hot wheat and wet leaves and the sight of sun on a creek or a puddle, and the sound of cicadas and magpies.

There were miles of brownish heather, the purple blooms faded, and bracken and short wiry grasses and rocky outcrops. The moors were high and wild and the vegetation had a roughness of texture. Even with villages scattered in the dales, the uplands felt untamed and a little disturbing, as if they were tugging at the threads on the edges of a well-made life. The walks though, were along the river valleys: green and patterned with meadows and fields. We stayed in a pub in the village of Grassington, which it turned out was only 30 kilometres from where the Brontës had lived.

When I looked at my Yorkshire notes, there were only a few

images: 'Fields, woods, stone walls, intense green pastures, oaks, chestnuts, birches, pines, then beyond, the harsh brown of old heather.'

I stared at the scribbled words and at first felt blank, but when I found the map of the walk, whole sections came back to me. This happens when I write about walking – a walk, which at first has only the barest outline in memory, comes back into detailed step-by-step life as if an interior film starts playing. I walk along whole sections in my mind and see my boot leap onto a particular stone, the diagonal path across a long rectangular field and the sheep huddling at one end. Neuroscientists suggest fragments of memory – a smell, a sight, a sound – are stored in various sites in the brain which the hippocampus, a curled seahorse in the middle of the brain, puts together into a coherent image or story when one fragment is triggered by a context. It means all that's needed is one scent, one word, one sensation of a stone underfoot for a sequence to reconstruct then replay.

Perhaps everything you have done is stored somewhere in the labyrinth of memory and only needs the right key to make it suddenly spring into an astonishing virtual world, like Proust's Combray, and the Guermantes and Méséglise ways, his Sunday walks, unfolding out of the eternal crumb of madeleine cake dipped in lime-flower tea. Apparently many memories are lost; some events do not make the neural pathway fire strongly or often enough to form a permanent image and I have to admit that days, months, even years of my life are blank, or at least misty, but I want to believe that I could, if I applied myself to the task, find the original flickering synaptic current. The fear is always that what is unremembered is pointless. The fact that it happened is never enough.

# The JOY of HIGH PLACES

We walked along a stone-walled footpath outside of Grassington, fields on one side, woods on the other. The sky was cloudy, rain threatening, but the air was still. I put my hand on the spongy moss covering the stone wall, thicker and softer than emerald velvet. The scene was more Blyton than Brontë but it did feel as if nothing had changed for centuries. There were fields with a few sheep, tussocky hillsides, scattered oaks, and, in the distance, rough moorland with brown heather patches. Every hundred metres or so there were stiles, mostly made of stone, sometimes wooden. We came to a group of Dutch walkers, talking as they climbed one after the other through one of the narrow stone stiles. I have an image of a large bottom in orange shorts turning sideways trying to squeeze through and everyone else trying not to look, as well as an ungenerous feeling – in me – of judgment not just of her, but of everyone in the group. They were about my age, on the other side of 50, and were clearly devoted to walking, but I didn't want to talk to them or even acknowledge them. I don't like walking in groups because I don't want to feel as if I ought to talk. I walk with Anthony but we rarely speak; it's as if we are each walking separately. I disappear – as I imagine he does – into an interior landscape of memory and reverie.

Some walkers declare the only true walking is alone. Robert Louis Stevenson said it had to be done alone, and Goethe and Baudelaire walked alone – but perhaps they didn't have anyone with whom they could walk silently. Why have rules about how walking should be done? And then I remember the Dutch walkers and wonder why I felt that my walking was somehow superior to theirs. Of anything that humans can do, surely walking is an expression of equality. It needs no particular skill or intelligence or fitness or knowledge or money; it requires only one foot after the other, each time finding the surface of the earth, toes absorbing pressure, arms slightly swinging, balance perpetually adjusting to keep the body vertical. A moment-by-moment miracle of evolution on a short walk through the Yorkshire Moors.

Still, miracle or not, walking is slow. If you are in a hurry, if you want something to happen quickly, there's no pleasure in walking. It's not a fast-paced narrative, it unfolds in moments – a moth breaking out of a chrysalis, a cow staring with unfathomable eyes – the texture of the world is constantly under your fingertips. It always takes me a while to slow down to a walking pace.

Walking undoes hierarchies too. When I walk, nothing is more important than anything else. The mountain doesn't mean any more than a chrysalis or any more than my own past; each one is absorbing. It doesn't feel anarchic, nor lacking in climactic moments; it's more that there's no hero. I am just part of the story.

After reaching the tiny village of Burnsall, we returned along the river Wharfe, past an old water mill and through a gorge where teenagers were jumping off a high bridge into the water. The clouds were shifting and reforming, making patterns of light and shade on the river and fields. The river most of the way was lined with horse chestnut trees, and conkers littered the path. I didn't know what they were but Anthony said he used to play 'conkers' as a child in New Zealand – they would tie a conker to a piece of string and hit at each other's until one broke.

'We had our own language for it,' he said, 'but I can't remember. I think there were *none-ers* when you had not beaten anyone.'

'Like marbles,' I said. 'I remember *taws* that we used to knock the other marbles out. And the really big ones were *stonkers*. And I liked the *cats eyes*.'

The words brought the feel of the marbles back to me, the smoothness of the glass ones and the slight roughness of stone marbles that had been chipped from rough play.

We talked all the way back to Grassington, indulging in the sweetness of reminiscing as the words brought back the lived feel of the past. They wove a kind of transparent fabric around us, creating the past in the present without any disjunction, but I didn't see much of anything around me.

We walked in Cornwall along the coast for three days, and then in the Cotswolds, leaving the oldest path in England to last. The Ridgeway is around 5000 years old, and was used as a trading route by the Celts and then Romans, Saxons, Vikings and by the English right up through medieval times and later. It's part of the Icknield Way that originally ran from the Salisbury Plains to East Anglia. Because it was high, dry ground it was easier to drive stock along and, in times of war, the long outlook made it easy to see danger.

There are much older walking paths in Australia, used by the Wiradjuri and other Indigenous peoples. In 1817 a Wiradjuri man led the early English explorer John Oxley along a Wiradjuri path to the site where my hometown was established 200 years ago. And the Bundian Way, 365 kilometres over the Snowy Mountains from the Monaro country in the west to the eastern coast, was used by the Yuin, Ngarigo, Bidhawal and Monaro peoples. It pre-dates the Ridgeway by tens of thousands of years, but this and most other paths were obscured by two centuries of English settlement. In the last few years the Bundian Way and other Indigenous paths have been rediscovered and work has begun clearing and preparing them for walking again. These are the paths of ancient Australia and I long one day to walk them, putting my feet on the earth where others have walked for millennia.

There is a communion in it, a deep intimacy, to put your foot exactly where another traveller has. It is safer, of course, the ground already tried and been proved secure, no hole or bog to fall into, but it is also a kind of marriage, foot on foot; you have both connected to the earth in the same place. I don't think I have the true explorer's desire to walk where no-one else has. Penetrating virgin country has no appeal; why be first? To walk in the footsteps of my Celtic ancestors, to put my twenty-first century feet on the earth, on the rock, where my ancestors did, was what I wanted.

We had time to walk the first 17 kilometres of the Ridgeway from Avebury to Ogbourne St George. Just before the beginning of the path is the Avebury stone *henge*, a circular bank with a ditch on the inside, and *sarsens*, a ring of hard sandstone monuments, making three circles. It's assumed the henge was used for rituals, although there's still no way of knowing what the rituals or their purpose were. The stones are variously shaped, not regular like those at Stonehenge, each one seeming to have an individual significance. They are solid, ancient, imposing, but goats were grazing nearby and houses were scattered about so that the scene looked homely. The stones have been there for over 5000 years, which, compared to Australian Indigenous artefacts, is not so long. I wondered why I had come so far to experience ancient connection when it was right there in my homeland.

The trail proper began at Overton Hill, just outside Avebury. Almost immediately Silbury Hill rose on the right, a Neolithic mound more than 40 metres high, similar in height to a smaller Egyptian pyramid. Archaeological evidence suggests that it was begun around 2400 BC but no-one knows why. It's made of chalk and clay and would have taken many people many years to build – one archaeologist estimated 500 labourers working daily for 15 years. It had been thought to be a burial mound, but recent research has shown there are no human remains at its core, just more clay and turf and freshwater shells, oak and hazel wood, sarsen stones and a few ox bones and antlers.

The trail led upwards for a while and then we were on the ridge itself, with a view over the rolling Wiltshire countryside. It didn't create the wild-hearted excitement of high places, but a sense of safety and expansive ease. We passed coppices, spinneys, thickets, copses and groves. The word *bucolic* came to mind – a word that seems only to apply to English countryside – like the names on the map: Ogbourne Maizey, Winterbourne Bassett, Miltonhall.

The trail continued along the ridge, flat and easy – it wasn't difficult to see why ridges were the quickest and safest way to get anywhere – and arrived at the Barbary Fort, one of several forts built along it in the Iron Age – between 800 BC and 100 AD. It had two defensive ditches and ramparts, and originally there were more than 40 dwellings within it. As I wandered over the ditches and ramparts an unexpected dreaminess drifted in. It was the kind of reverie that comes unbidden, most often while reading or walking. I'm not sure that reverie is actually the right word. It feels ungraspable and I can't call it back at will. Even if I go back to certain places, or re-read phrases in an effort to call it back, it won't work. That day it fell around me like an intensely pleasurable drug. There was stillness and strength somewhere under the heart; my mind was dreamy, as if in a trance, but sights and smells of the autumn day were heightened.

I have wondered about these kind of experiences of unbidden reverie or joy, especially when they come from a particular place elsewhere in the world. There's no childhood memory to influence my response and yet there is something unthought happening. I don't attribute it to God or anything otherworldly but I do accept the possibility of inherited cellular memory of place. Who can say how time works. Thoughts drifted with images of the men and women and children who had lived here more than 2000 years ago, but at the same time I could see a dandelion clock moving in the breeze, hear a bee buzzing, feel the softness of the meadow grass under my boots.

We stayed there at Barbary Fort for a long time, and in the end only left because Anthony said we had to keep going if we wanted to get to Ogbourne St George before dark. I felt the place pulling me back as I turned and walked away along the ridge.

Further along the ridge the gravel path was lined with late summer grasses and herbs – yarrow, dandelions, blackberries, rye grass, a few bluebells and buttercups. The path stretched out in front, flat and clear, not even a gully or rocks to adjust my gait to. In the days when my ancestors walked it, it must have been uneven, scattered with stones and tree roots, scuffed by cattle and sheep and horses.

It was late afternoon when we arrived at Ogbourne

# The JOY of HIGH PLACES

St George, where we stayed the night before I had to leave to work in Paris. I wrote in my notebook:

> If only I could keep walking, then I would find whatever it is I'm looking for. It feels like a compulsion, like a love affair, or the search for God. Am I looking for answers, something outside of myself? Is it the occasional hit of enchantment – an addict's desire to live only for the dreamy high? The moment of revelation?

By the time I was a teenager, the walks across the paddocks and up to Baron Rock, a volcanic outcrop behind the farm, hinted at revelation. I didn't ever have to walk far before the feeling rose like an invisible vibration and shimmered around me. It was more than reverie; it contained a promise. This feeling, which first arrived then, has often happened when I walk in the Australian bush, but never anywhere else. It's only the promise of revelation, never fulfilled, but it's enough to keep me coming back.

I don't remember walking much with Barney except to Baron Rock and to school with my other brothers and younger sister. When I picture him, there's an air of separateness from all the rest of us. He's listening to his transistor radio, or doing his homework, or painting neat, accurate pictures, often secluded at his end of the sleep-out. When we sat around the fire in winter, he liked to pose worrying questions: what if we are all just in someone's dream and one day they will wake up and we won't exist? And then he didn't believe in God anymore and didn't seem to care what anyone thought about that. Without being able to say so, I sensed he was made of ideas, rather than feelings, but perhaps I was noticing that he was no longer a child and I still was.

By the time we were both young adults, a mutual avoidance was well established. Our paths had diverged almost as soon as we left school. I was a hippy, living under canvas in the Sunburst commune in the wet New Zealand bush with Anthony, and in large share houses in the city. Wherever I lived, Nature was the highest good; the way of the natural world was law. I stopped taking the contraceptive pill and let nature take its course, so that I was literally barefoot and pregnant before I was 21. I padded around the land with my round belly, feeling the dirt beneath my feet and the soft rain on my hair and face. The week before my first son was born, I walked the four kilometres along Gentle Annie Road, a gravel track from the commune to the main road, to hitchhike to Auckland. It was a short walk, but a significant one. My belly was ungainly and my home-made sandals kept turning on the gravel and I was so young – I must have caused anyone who saw me to worry for my future – and yet I felt like someone in procession, carrying a new life into the world like millennia of women before me. I was barely more than a teenager and I was already walking into the next part of my life.

Barney, the few times I saw him, thought I was weird in my long loose dresses with my long loose hair, non–meat eating habits and dope-smoking share households. I thought he was too narrow, too controlled, going off to teach at primary school in his suit and tie every day. It didn't look as if our paths would cross much anymore, and for years, they didn't.

# Gods and monks

And then one day, decades after leaving the farm, in a change of direction that startled all of us, Barney stopped going to work and started to fly. It was nearly as simple as that. He took paragliding lessons, bought a second-hand glider and off he flew. He became one of the bird-people.

There have been many bird-people in mythology and in history, earthbound creatures who wanted to fly. They used feathers and wax and paper and glue and string, and they leapt off towers and abbeys and longed for transcendence. Mostly they died. Sometimes they ended up as stars, living in the sky world forever.

Why did they risk their lives to soar in the sky, and why have I remained earth-bound? I walk on the earth, step by step, let the earth spin under my feet. My brother stepped off the sides of mountains into the air. He defied gravity, let the air currents hold him above the earth. Like a creature in a myth or dream, he took to the realm of the gods. It makes me wonder about the human desire for flight, where it came from, how it grew.

In many places around the world there are myths of humans flying. In the stories of Indigenous Australians, there were two brothers from the Adnyamathanha people of the northern Flinders Ranges, who were caught by a bushfire on top of a rocky mountain. There was no way out and they screamed in fear. The conflagration was of their own making – they had lit a small fire to smoke the flies away from an emu they had caught – but the flames had roared up around them. The Ancestors took pity on them and gave them the gift of flight. The brothers flew into the sky where they realised they were safe at last. They made their camp there in the sky and every night everyone can see their campfires, the two pointers of the Southern Cross.

For the Wiradjuri, the original people of the land where Barney and I grew up, the world is divided into halves, or moieties, represented by birds: the eaglehawk and the crow. Every Wiradjuri is one or other of these birds in their soul. I remember Rose Chown, a local woman from my hometown, who told me she 'would come back as an eaglehawk … because [he] flies up so high he's detached from everything … he must have some wisdom about all this'. Both birds were always there in my childhood: the crow presaged death to me – oh, it stole eggs and it picked out the eyes of newborn lambs – and the eaglehawk was freedom and wildness as it floated on air currents in the distant blue above the farm.

On the other side of the world in ancient Greece, Pegasus, the flying horse with glowing white wings, soared through the heavens. Pegasus was caught, tamed and ridden in the skies by the human, Bellerophon. Together they defeated the Chimera with its lion head, goat body and serpent-headed tail, but eventually Bellerophon was dashed to earth by Zeus for thinking he could match the gods. Pegasus, like the Adnyamathanha brothers, was changed into a constellation in the night sky.

# The JOY of HIGH PLACES

It was in mythic Greece too, that Daedalus constructed wings from feathers and wax so that he and his son Icarus could escape the labyrinth in which they were imprisoned. We all know he told his exuberant son not to fly too near the sun, the abode of the gods, as he carefully attached the wings with wax. But Icarus didn't listen. He flew too high, the wax melted, the wings collapsed and he fell to his death. Ah now, ah now, don't fly too high, don't forget you are an earth creature, don't forget your limits even in the midst of joy.

Jewish and Christian angels could fly from heaven to earth and back again, whenever they liked. How I loved them when I was a child: the seraphim – fiery beings with six wings – and cherubim, dominions and principalities, angels and archangels, all of them with splendid feathered wings curving over their heads. There was a guardian angel too, one assigned to watch over each and every one of us, always pictured on holy cards standing just behind a child – me – walking on the edge of a river or cliff. Guardian angels were male but had feminine faces and wore flowing robes and mostly had white wings, although some had crimson, green and blue wings like human rosellas.

In African cultures, both before and after people were seized and transported to the Americas, stories of humans flying were widespread. 'Flying African' myths could be seen as a reaction to slavery, a way of escape, but flying stories already existed in pre-slavery Africa. In the words of a traditional African American spiritual, 'I got wings, you got wings, all God's chillun got wings'. One of the stories, 'All God's Children Had Wings' begins 'Once all Africans could fly like birds', and immediately I found myself believing it.

In Egyptian mythology the god Thoth took the form of a

bird, an ibis. He is often pictured with an ibis head, although sometimes as a whole ibis with bird wings and feet. He was the god of wisdom, writing, mathematics and magic – and as if that were not enough, he also took charge of the judgment of the dead. He served as the scribe of the gods, and is said to have invented the alphabet itself. If a bird-god invented the alphabet, then that seems to connect flight with written words. Written language was first employed for inventories and recording deals, but it would soon be used to inscribe stories on clay tablets for the first time, preserving them from the vagaries of human memory.

But humans weren't content to leave flight to gods and angels and mythic creatures. With our thick legs and bulky bodies, we have no physical characteristic that makes us fit for flight, which makes me think there must be something in our neurophysiology that creates the desire to step off the earth, to see it from above. Of course it could just be that watching the graceful flight of birds made us long to emulate them, but it turns out that walking and flying may not be so very far apart. Ethnologists have recently suggested that the desire to fly was born when we first began to walk upright. The human sense of balance developed at the same time – we needed that to stay upright on two precarious feet – and our sense of being in space, along with the ability to imagine other perspectives, predisposed us to the idea of flight. And then two or three adventurers walked up a mountain out of the Great Rift Valley in Africa and looked back and saw what might be possible, what vistas could open up, if only they could fly. The idea was born.

I don't mean to write a whole history of the human efforts to fly, but long before Barney, there were many people through the centuries who yearned to be birdmen. I couldn't find any records of winged women leaping off towers and mosques and castle walls, but 50 or so men have been recorded. In Andalusia, in the ninth century, the Muslim inventor, Abbas ibn Firnas, covered himself in feathers, attached wings to his body and flung himself into the air – it's not recorded whether from a building or cliff – and, according to reports, flew a considerable distance but broke his back when he landed. In the eleventh century, an English monk, Eilmer, attached feathers to his arms and leapt from the top of Malmesbury Abbey. He was airborne for about 15 seconds before he landed and broke both his legs.

There were many more attempts, all of them hopeful and hopeless, before various men came up with flying machines, but machines with wings are not the same as winged humans. A mechanical means of flying, even da Vinci's elegant ornithopter, separates humans from the physical act of flying; the body is not involved. A paragliding wing, however, dependent on air currents and human skill to stay wing-shaped, is an extension of the body. It responds to each movement of the torso and arms; the long lines are like nerves relaying messages all along the edges of the wing. You become, in fact, a winged human.

There are various competing stories about who thought of paragliding first. Some claim it was the French parachute designer Pierre Lemoigne, whose 'gliding parachute', designed in 1962, was modified in 1978 by three Frenchmen – Bosson, Bétemps and Bohn – and renamed a 'parapente'. It was first used by walkers and climbers in the Alps as a faster way down from the summits rather than abseiling perilously over cliffs. I like the idea that the wing originated from the desire to fly down a mountain after walking and climbing up over rocks and snow and ice, but the strongest claim for its origins is the 'sail wing', designed by an American, David Barish.

In the odd way the world works, Barish was not working on a way of lifting off, of flying, but on a way of landing safely – he was designing and testing ways of recovering space capsules for NASA. He soon realised his 'sail wing' could be used for human flight. He tried it himself at the Belleayre ski resort in the Catskill Mountains north of New York in September 1965, and finally on that day, a bulky, aerodynamically useless human lifted off the ground and flew without the use of a machine. Using only his wing, Barish flew over 100 metres down a ski slope and 'slope-soaring', as he called it, was born.

Barish was a keen skier and at first saw slope-soaring as a summer sport for ski resorts and he and his son took a trip across the country promoting it in the 1960s. 'We didn't know that it might be possible to soar in thermals or dynamic wind,' he remarked years later. It wasn't until the 1980s that the wing's potential for cross-country flight was realised and humans began to soar, dip and dive, spiral and hover, just like birds, for hundreds of kilometres. Barish was busy with his aeronautical work and didn't fly for years and didn't even realise until late in his life that the sport he had invented had literally taken off around the world. He took up paragliding again his seventies and flew until the year before he died at age 88.

I haven't been able to find out what Barish felt when he first flew like a bird. He was a modest man and wasn't acknowledged as the inventor of winged human flight during his life. His obituary in the *New York Times* in 2009 referred to him as 'the forgotten father of paragliding'. But I like to think that he would have echoed Barney's words in the Fountain cafe: 'I soared upwards, swooped and turned into the wind and hovered like a hawk. To move to the left I just leaned my body and off I flew. And then when I pulled my hands down, it was as if my wings were curving downwards and I slowed down, like a bird, to land.' And his whole body must have laughed for joy.

# Icarus

I've been reading the information Barney has sent me. There are dates and times, longitude and latitude, figures, technical terms, photographs. Every time I ask a simple question requiring a yes or no answer, I receive at least a page of notes. They make me smile – they are so well ordered compared to my messy pile of notebooks. Some things don't change; we will always go about things differently. Still, the facts in his story matter. I can't just draw a smudgy impressionistic line and let that stand for what happened to him. Tracing his journey on the map requires precision; it's a disciplined cartographer's job, I can see that. What is needed is a transcription of all the detail, exactly as recorded, onto a sky-map. I don't have a template for it because there are no permanent sky-maps, only maps of barometric pressure that change every day, so it will have to be a transient map that applies to only one day. The day he fell.

The day that Barney fell out of the sky, 22 September 2011, he took off from Beechmont hill in southern Queensland, at 28°7'3"

South, 153°12'7" East. I haven't been there, but I can visualise the launch site because Barney painted one of his accurate pictures of it, photographed the painting and emailed it to me. It was an oil painting – he likes working in oil because of its ability to represent lifelike textures – showing a grassy slope curving gently down at first, then more steeply into a basin with a stand of eucalypts on the right, more cleared paddocks below and a view out to rugged, bush-covered mountains. He painted three paragliders into the scene; the closest one is red with a black and white zigzag. The painting is neat and precise, a record rather than an interpretation.

It was a sunny, mostly blue-sky day with a few fluffy cumulus clouds. He had checked the meteorological report online as usual, noting barometric pressures and wind speeds in particular, and checked the weather station at Nerang, and the rain radar and the Doppler wind radar at nearby Mt Stapylton, and there was nothing concerning to note. Visibility was good; the visual flight rules mean you have to be able to see at least five kilometres to launch. The expected maximum temperature was 23 degrees and no rainfall was forecast. There had been a fall of 14 millimetres nearly two weeks before, which meant the countryside was soft with new grass – this is an important detail to note. He had checked the gliding forecast site for buoyancy/shear ratio of wind, and thermal strength and range of gust strength before he left home and now that he was here he could feel the light south-east breeze, under 15 km/h, coming up the hill towards the launch site – a necessary condition as air needs to be flowing uphill to launch successfully.

He had dropped Jenny off at Brisbane airport on his way to Beechmont. She was flying out to Adelaide to visit her elderly father for a few days. Their three adult children were spread around the world, in Auckland, Budapest and Dubai, all of them enjoying adventurous lives, none of them concerned about their 61-year-old father leaping off into the sky that day.

He had been flying for six years by then and was confident in his skills and in his equipment, his red Nova Mentor 2 with its black and white zigzag pattern. He had methodically checked the *canopy* for tears, the *lines* (fine ropes) and *risers* (webbing straps) for tangles, and the *carabiners* (clips attaching risers to the harness) and the *altimeter-variometer* (which indicates height and rate of rise or fall) to make sure all was well. He had gained a reputation for being so thorough and knowledgeable about the technical aspects of flying, and about weather conditions in particular, that other flyers rang him to find out what was forecast rather than check the Bureau of Meteorology site themselves.

He sat on the hillside with about a dozen flying friends, mostly men and a couple of women, enjoying the warmth of the early spring sun and the companionship of being able to exchange stories about *cloud-suck*, *thermal triggers*, *B-line stall*, *kiting*, *anti-G chutes* and *ridge-soaring* with people who knew what he was talking about. They called sitting on the hill *para-waiting*, which makes me smile again. Their waiting was not like other people's amorphous waiting; it was formed into a specific shape around their joy and had its own pleasure.

Sitting with them gave him an easy companionship he had never known before. I didn't see him much in his twenties or thirties, but he didn't seem to have any close friends or even mates to hang out with at the pub. In fact, he never went to the pub. He and Jenny married young and he didn't seem to need anyone else; there still seemed to be a desire to stay apart from the general foolishness of human beings. When his children were young, he didn't celebrate birthdays or Christmases because such celebrations weren't rational. It put a bit of a damper on ordinary conversational exchange at the times of year families might be expected to be in contact. Conversation at any time was awkward. I used to think it was individualism based on feeling superior, but I've since realised it was because he didn't have anything he wanted to say. He told me lately that he had always felt like a misfit socially, but now that he had found his passion, what he was born for, he could sit and talk about it happily with other flyers for hours. He felt more comfortable on the hillside than at any other time or place in his life.

The breeze was light, the air was warm, but not hot, the windsock lifted gently and the grass rippled a little. A few magpies flew steadily without being buffeted. Several other paragliders had taken off – Jason, Al, Kirsty, Bridgette – and it was now Barney's turn. There's a wide launch area at Beechmont, wide enough for six to take off at once, which was useful during competitions, but this Thursday morning was just for pleasure; there was no rush. From his reading of the conditions, he expected to climb to over 4000 feet and then fly for about 50 kilometres, perhaps westwards towards Beaudesert where he knew some good landing spots.

He spent 20 minutes getting ready. He unzipped the harness and wing from the backpack and attached his reserve – a lightweight parachute for emergencies – and instruments to the harness: a flight computer (about the size of a large mobile phone), a 3D GPS, altimeter, variometer, compass, thermal tracker, ground-speed indicator, map, wind speed and direction indicator and flight recorder, a VHF radio, an ordinary magnetic ball compass (in case of being sucked up into a cloud, where a computer screen is hard to read) and the SPOT tracker and emergency beacon. Then, along with his sandwiches, he put the 'camel pack' in the storage area of the harness and threaded the tube through to the shoulder strap so that he could drink during the flight.

When Barney described this whole process to me – my mind blurring with the detail – it was suddenly obvious that his technical brain and methodical nature formed the necessary base for all this flying off into blue sky romance. The equipment had to be assessed and used with precise care, every action had to be done in sequence and checked and rechecked, all the information about conditions had to be gathered and understood. If you didn't, you might leave the ground, but you wouldn't last long. It wasn't just a matter of an ignominious tumble; it was life and death. He was willing to face it, but without the slightest trace of recklessness. I had never understood before the clear relationship between rigorous discipline and utter freedom.

I had decided to keep out of Barney's story, to let him have the stage, as they say, but I have begun to realise I am in it anyway. I'm selecting and reshaping his responses to my relentless questions – and I can't help reacting as well. I don't mean to be a Greek chorus, but I keep being astonished by him. His disciplined, methodical nature is so unlike mine – I am always being excited by wonders – and yet I am learning awe from him, a strange emotion buried deep in humans. It's the same feeling I used to have as a child watching a chick peck its way out of an egg. The perfect smooth surface cracked and something showed through, just a murky bit of feather, or a blobby eye, but once it started, I'd have to keep watching until the end, until the new unsteady creature was in the world. I felt lucky, so lucky, to have been there at the right time, I wasn't going to keep quiet about it.

Barney continued the process in easy movements. Next he spread the wing out, checking it over and making sure all the lines were clear, then put his harness on loosely and connected the risers by clipping them into the carabiners. Then he bunched up the wing and put it aside with the harness while he put on his helmet and parka and attached his UHF radio to a PTT mic/speaker system inside his helmet for communicating with other flyers and with his retrieve driver at the end of the flight, and put the radio in his jacket pocket. He already had his hiking boots on – they were heavier than ordinary shoes but they provided stability and ankle support for landing.

Now he was ready to clip in. He put his arms through the shoulder straps and clipped on the T-strap style leg loop, then bent down and looped a bungy under his heel to keep the bottom of the harness in place so he could easily get his feet into it once airborne – a retractable undercarriage! He then did up the 'fail-safe' leg loop system as a double insurance against falling out of the harness, and then clipped the chest strap shut. Finally, he put his gloves on, did a radio check to make sure it was working, picked up the wing and carried it across to the launching area.

The wing lay on the grass behind him. One of his flying friends, Drew, helped spread it, and he could feel the slight weight of the harness on his shoulders. He went through a mental checklist of everything he had just done to make sure he hadn't forgotten anything. He gripped the *A risers* attached to the leading edge of the wing in his right hand and pulled gently, which opened the leading edge and allowed the breeze to inflate the cells of the wing. He checked the lines to make sure they hadn't tangled again. The wing lifted as it inflated, until it rose above his head, and then he pulled down on the *C risers,* attached to the trailing edge, to prevent the wing surging over his head and collapsing in front of him. Getting the timing of the C risers right was one of the first things to master – you looked a bit silly when a wing collapsed on top of you before you had gone anywhere at all.

Flight is dependent on the caprice of the wind, even when everything has been done correctly. If the wind is light and variable, or a wind wafts from the back just as you attempt to launch, the wing will lose air speed, air will flow out of the cells instead of in, and the wing will collapse while you are running downhill at full tilt. There would be no other option except slithering on your bum down the slope to the *bomb-out* at the bottom of the hill. Today, though, the wind was light to moderate and flowing uphill: nothing to worry about.

Now that the wing was steady over his head, he checked that all the lines were tangle free and all adjusted to the right length. He held the brake handles in each hand under the riser straps, and then released the A and C risers, still holding onto the brakes, turned down the hill and slightly to the right, making sure he didn't twist the lines. The wing pulled forward and he walked to keep up with it, pulling the brakes a little to stop it surging over his head. Because the wind was light, he ran for a few steps and then the wing lifted him fluidly off the grassy ground, easily and gently, just like in his childhood dreams. Within an impossible moment he was as weightless as an angel.

# The JOY of HIGH PLACES

I look up from his notes. The lift-off! All the training, all the work and attention is for this moment. The split second in which the weight of the world loosens, when gravity lets go, when there is nothing holding you down. After that, there is still work to do, a wing to manage, speed and balance and direction to correct, but that first moment, that's pure intoxication. The scratch of harness, the heat and weight of boots, they are all gone. You are in another dimension, held up by wings that do not beat, but which keep you afloat without effort.

Barney pushed himself back into his pod harness as soon as he was airborne and slipped his feet into the cocoon, giving him a streamlined and comfortable position. The wing tugged, seeming to want to fly itself as it always did, to have a mind, or desire, of its own. It was swinging light, lazy pendulums; he corrected them by shifting and leaning a little against the swing. It was easy but he still needed to concentrate. Once, a few months earlier, he was caught in a sudden updraft as he took off and shot straight upwards like a skyrocket. That got his adrenalin pumping, he said. Even observing every detail, the invisible caprices of the air were not entirely predictable.

The slope was already metres beneath him, but he could still see blades of feathery spear grass, clover and native grasses, looking deceptively soft and thick. He leaned to the right and the wing dipped and turned towards the basin. The balance of his wing, its *pendular stability*, came from his body being the central weight of the pendulum, as if his body were the brass knob swinging on the end of a string. It meant the wing would continue to fly straight ahead and level if nothing else interfered;

direction could be changed using the left and right brakes or by leaning to the left or right. Pitch, roll and yaw – twisting or oscillating around the vertical axis – were controlled with either the brakes or lean.

The air was turbulent, buffeting the wing and his body sideways and upwards, jerking him around as if he were on a roller coaster. He headed towards the top of the ridge, looking for some thermal lift. He was about 150 feet above the eucalypts, close enough to see the detail of foliage and his friends' faces, high enough to see out across the ranges, but he wasn't looking towards them because he needed to concentrate on gaining height. He was aware of the blue haze of the mountains on the periphery of his vision, the light and shadow of peaks and valleys, and below, a smooth green carpet.

This was his country, the part of Australia where he had planned to live for years. His place, the house where he lived with Jenny on the edge of Murwillumbah, looking out over cane fields towards Mt Warning – Wollumbin or 'cloud-catcher' to the local Bundjalung people – was 50 kilometres away as the crow flies, as he could fly. It was on the other side of the Springbrook National Park; the road he drove on to the launch area snaked along the Nerang River, a brownish thread he could use as a geographical marker when he flew southwards.

This part of northern NSW and southern Queensland is subtropical, mountainous, wild, but also dotted with farmlands and towns – it is fertile and well-watered, green for most of the year. He felt at home there, felt connected to the calm, unthreatening landscape, although he had also felt he belonged in the dry central west when he was growing up there. He had not imagined or longed for anywhere else until he was an adult.

When he told me that, I felt disloyal that even as a child I had dreamed of elsewhere.

The valleys and mountains of Bundjalung country had attracted thousands of hippies looking for a sustainable life in the rainforest in the 1970s, and by the time Barney arrived with Jenny and their three children in the late 1980s, the region was dotted with communities that grew their own everything. Feral living in the bush without modern conveniences didn't really interest Barney, and the belief systems and practices – Gaia and goddesses and chakras – were as irrational to him as the religion he had rejected as a teenager. It's obvious from the paintings he did in his spare time – his choice of subjects: fields, houses, river, fences, backed by neat mountains and large skies – that he was drawn to orderly beauty and especially the linking of human and natural order. There was no starkness or wildness in his pictures, but a sure appreciation, almost an imprisonment, of a safe and pleasing world.

Above the earth, it looked different, especially when he was thousands of feet high. Geographic features were easy to see, but mountains and hills seemed flatter and lower from above. He was often surprised to find a landing area quite steep when from higher up it had appeared to be flat. Usually he flew at between 3000 and 7000 feet – flyers measure height in feet rather than metres – and one day he reached 9500 feet in a thermal. He could have gone higher but he wasn't carrying oxygen – any higher than 10 000 feet and flyers are legally required to be on oxygen. It sounded terrifying to me to be so far above the earth with only a slim arc of nylon holding me up, but he said the higher the better.

'It's much safer than being close to the ground – if

something goes wrong there is plenty of time to either sort it out, or throw the reserve,' he said. 'There's also more time to find the next thermal and more chance of reaching it if it's far away. And,' he added, 'the view from up there is more spectacular'.

When I pushed him to tell me why he did it, what he really got out of it apart from the great view, at first he gave me evolutionary theory. That is, we are hard-wired to enjoy anything that develops survival skills, giving us an evolutionary edge – mobility, speed, dexterity, problem solving and especially the ability to use the forces of nature to achieve our own purposes. Flying did all of that. Then he'd realised from the look on my face that I wanted something more personal and grinned and said 'Flying makes me feel good. I mean really, really good!! Happy, excited, stimulated, amazed.'

Afterwards he wrote, trying to explain his experience more precisely:

> The feelings of just flying around, turning, swooping, skimming over the trees, floating along under a cumulus cloud, circling with soaring birds, landing softly or taking off from a hillside, are all thrilling physical and emotional sensations. When I lock into the core of a thermal there is a 'yes!' feeling and at the top I feel triumphant and then, immediately re-focused on what I need to do next. When the conditions are good, it is also a very liberating feeling to be able to just choose where I want to go and then fly there.

He sent me a photograph of himself as a dot in the sky under a red and white wing. There was blue sky all around him and clouds beneath, then, far below, a farming landscape patterned with cloud shadows and, in the distance, mountains and a far blue horizon. He said he had often thought of painting the view from up there, 'but to do it justice', he said, 'it would have to be painted on the inside of a large sphere and viewed from the inside'.

When he said that, it made me realise how being up there, floating in the sky, gave him the sense of being in a 360-degree reality. When I've reached the highest pass walking across mountains, I have gained some sense of that: the great dome of the sky above and the land below. Of course, everyone on the planet is in that reality, but with the solid earth beneath our feet, I suppose we see in horizontal and vertical planes. He was inside the egg of the world, a tiny speck of matter at the beginning of the infinite universe, soaring and circling above the curved earth.

On this day though, he was still only about 200 feet up, trying to climb using the usually reliable thermal triggers along the ridge. He had been circling for a while and it was starting to feel like he wasn't going anywhere today. He knew from experience it would become fatiguing to keep pulling on the brakes on the turns when the rising air was weak. A series of punchy thermal bullets, narrow columns of rising warm air, lifted him, but then he lost them and flew into a moderate sink of falling cool air. It was hard work and nothing he tried was getting him any further ahead. Flying wasn't about wandering in a dreamy fashion; it was a focused seeking of invisible paths. Today wasn't going to be the day he soared above the glorious world chatting to wedge-tailed eagles.

He decided to head back in for a landing on the bomb-out and try again later on. Sometimes, as the afternoon progressed, there were better thermals and cloud-suck – the lift created under clouds by the latent heat of evaporation released during condensation – so it could be worth sitting back on the hill and para-waiting for a while. He turned back and flew towards the bomb-out from the direction of the launch site for a clear approach, away from the stands of gum trees at the bottom. There were still plenty of punchy updrafts, so he was alert for any sudden changes. A sudden strong updraft near landing could collapse the wing and leave him in a very dangerous position.

He slid his legs out of the pod, ready for landing, and made a wide 180-degree turn for his final approach. He scanned the trees and the grass for any signs of unusual movement, especially the sudden flutter of dry leaves and dust on the ground, but the soft green regrowth from the recent rains gave nothing away.

He glided in gently and was in the middle of the landing site, just a few metres above the ground, when he was suddenly shot straight upwards in a violent twisting corkscrew of air. He realised afterwards it was a whirlwind, or dust-devil, but without the tell-tale dust – the short spring grass had hidden the signs. But at that moment there was no thought, only the sensation of his body being spun upwards in a nightmare whirl. The wild twisting upthrust caused a total collapse of the wing and the force of the swiftly rising air was so fierce he kept going upwards, reaching about 40 feet, the height of a four-storey building. He was at the same height as the wing itself as it tried to disentangle and re-open. The lines were slack and the leading edge of the wing was pointing towards the ground as it began to reinflate – and then it collapsed again. There was no time to reopen the wing or use his reserve. From four storeys up, he plummeted, feet first, towards the ground.

'Just eternal blackness now,' he thought. It was the only thing in his head, he told me later. Since his teenage rejection of religion, he had refused the comfort of any kind of afterlife, any kind of God. Now, as he faced eternal non-existence, he didn't change his mind.

As he braced himself for impact, he made one almighty effort and *flared*, pulled on the brakes of the just-reopening wing, as hard as he could a second before hitting the ground. That last-second flare changed the angle of impact from 90 to 60 degrees – and saved his life.

'I hit the ground very hard,' he told me later in an email. Every time I read that comment, I think he deserves some sort of award for understatement. Dropping to the ground from four floors up, I imagine you would hit very hard.

His legs buckled instantly and the bottom of his spine hit the ground with tremendous force. He felt two large bangs, like firecrackers going off in his back. His first thought was a surprised recognition that he was still alive. No eternal blackness. Then he realised he couldn't feel or move anything from the waist down and knew immediately that his back was broken. At that moment he was sure he would never walk again.

His injuries, later catalogued, were: a burst fracture of the T12 vertebra with shards damaging spinal nerves; stable fractures of the T2, T4 and S5; a chip off a higher vertebra; two broken ribs; severely bruised and battered feet, ankles and knees; nerve damage in the right hip and leg; and trauma to the lower bowel and bladder.

He didn't know any of that yet. He was alive and had to get help. Although the upper half of his body was in severe pain, he could move his torso and arms. He took his gloves off and pulled his radio out of his flight-suit pocket, and called for help. He can remember exactly what he said.

'This is Barney. I'm in the bomb-out. I've crashed. My back is broken. I can't move or feel anything from the waist down. I need help.'

There was no reply. He realised the radio must have changed channels in the crash, so he took his glasses from his pocket, changed the channel and called again. This time he received a reassuring response from Jason, who was flying nearby.

While he waited, he tried to detach his wing but the carabiners were under him, impossible to reach. He could see other flyers, Drew first and then Jason, spiralling down from the cloud-base to land beside him, so he waited. But the dust-devil suddenly showed its truly diabolic nature, returning and switching directions, instantly re-inflating his wing. He was picked up and swung along with just his toes touching the ground, dumped down again, then dragged, broken-backed, for 40 metres before he could pull down on the risers and bring the wing back under control. Now his gloveless hands were burned red-raw from pulling on the strings to save himself from the dreadful battering.

I find this moment, the dragging after the fall, more unspeakable than anything else. The fall is terrifying to think of, but the broken-backed dragging is sheer horror. It seems a stroke of extreme malice, even for the Fates who care less than nothing for any of us. Just leave it at flinging the body to earth, why don't you?

Drew landed and unclipped his own wing then ran towards him, followed by Jason and then Kirsty, Al and Bridgette. They knelt beside him, asked him foolishly if he was all right. They told him to lie perfectly still. Gavin, who had stayed back at the launch site, contacted the ambulance and coordinated messages from other emergency services – but didn't yet let Jenny know. Barney wanted to know what he was facing first. He had survived when he thought he was about to die and didn't know whether that was a good thing or not.

'This has actually happened,' he kept thinking as his mind struggled to make what had previously been an imaginary situation, into a real one, presenting it over and over. Soon, but not yet, the idea would stop slipping off the shiny surface of consciousness and gain the bleak texture of reality.

He would be a paraplegic for the rest of his life. His brain circled relentlessly over the many things he would never do again; the reality of not being able to stand, walk, run, dance, have sex, fly, or even go to the toilet. No more wandering in the sky, nor on the earth. The loss of independence. Being in a wheelchair forever and being a burden to Jenny. He dreaded having to tell her the news. And then he felt grateful that at least it didn't happen while Mum was alive; it would have been too distressing for her to bear.

I have to say this last remark reveals more than anything else how limited my knowledge of my brother had been in the past. To feel gratitude for sparing someone else pain at such a moment strikes me as extraordinary. Then I remember when our mother was dying the year before, he made the ten-hour drive from his home in Murwillumbah to Wellington to be with her during her last days. Kevin, our younger brother and a Buddhist, was there at the same time. We had a roster, all of us taking turns to sleep in her room and tend to her every hardly-existent need. Kevin rang me one day while Barney was out, praising his gentle and loving care of Mum.

'He gives her a little spoonful of mashed banana and a little sip of water, and he wipes her face and holds her hand.'

I was surprised, as I was meant to be. Even mentioning it carried the subtext: 'We didn't expect this of Barney did we, huh?' I hadn't been the only one in the family to build a simple and inaccurate picture of him.

He lay on the soft grass while the others gave him water, talked to him and held his wing over him for shade. He was dressed for high altitude and realised he felt too hot in the midst of the extreme pain. He clenched his teeth and waited. The others kept talking to him, reassuring him that things were perhaps not as bad as they seemed and that help was already on the way. He said afterwards he couldn't begin to describe his gratitude for the fact that his *comrades* – that's what he called them – were there with him.

'I never realised before how much we need other people to survive,' he said.

The ambulance arrived after about 40 minutes. The paramedics asked him questions and tried to diagnose his injuries but didn't give him any painkillers – when spinal cord injuries are suspected, painkillers are withheld because the medication can interfere with the specialist's diagnosis. He kept clenching his teeth while the paramedics cut him out of his wing and flying suit and then lifted and strapped him onto a stretcher. Twenty minutes later, the medical helicopter arrived. The doctor on board also didn't administer painkillers – and warned him that the helicopter would vibrate a lot as it revved up to take off and that it was going to hurt.

'He wasn't wrong,' Barney said.

Once they were airborne the flight was smooth and was

'okay'. Barney lay on his back staring at the padded ceiling while the doctor kept a close eye on him. They flew him to the specialist spinal unit at Brisbane's Princess Alexandra hospital, where the helicopter landed on the roof. Hospital staff, nurses and doctors, ran out and he was trolleyed to an emergency theatre, nurses plugging in electrodes and cannulas and doctors calling out directions and ordering equipment as they ran.

'Just like on TV shows,' Barney said.

The damage was quickly assessed. First, before the operation, Barney had to sign an indemnity form. The surgeon stressed that all he could do was to prevent the bone pieces from further cutting his spinal cord. Only time would tell, he said, the extent of the nerve damage and how much of it would repair. He hoped for the best, but he made clear that there was no guarantee Barney would walk again. He explained that as well as the danger of further damage to his spinal cord, there was a chance he could also lose his sight as a result of the operation.

The surgical team was introduced to him, which seems oddly polite in the circumstances – Barney says he remembers the introduction happening but not anyone's names. Then he was anaesthetised and the surgeon began the delicate five-hour operation on the shattered T12, the lowest thoracic vertebra at the inward curve of the spine. He pulled the shards of bone away from the spinal cord and stabilised it by binding it with titanium rods to the vertebrae above and below it. The T12 is in the region that sends messages to and from the legs, so that any hope of walking again depended on the success of this reconstruction. It was the evening of the day the accident happened and none of us yet knew any of this.

Auden wrote in 'Musée des Beaux Arts', his lovely poem on

# Icarus

Brueghel's painting of Icarus falling into the sea, that cataclysm and suffering happen 'While someone else is eating or opening a window or just walking dully along'. I'd had a quiet Thursday at home. It was our older son's birthday, but he had gone out with his girlfriend, and Anthony and I had walked along the waterfront near where we live to Mrs Macquarie's Chair. It was the usual short walk down the McElhone Stairs, across the wharves and along the harbourside under paperbark gums and banksia. Weathered sandstone created natural sculptures along one side of the walk; on the other the waves lapped against the sea wall as always. It was spring and grevilleas and bottlebrush were blossoming, but the evening was cool so we walked quickly.

When Kathy – the oldest in the family and a trained nurse – rang next morning, I knew from the tone of her voice something was wrong. She told me that Barney had had a flying accident, that he had broken his spine in several places and it looked like he wouldn't walk again. I remember thinking, Barney will never fly again. In those first moments, it seemed worse than the fact that he wouldn't walk again. And, of course, I thought about Icarus. The non-existent Gods would always have their way.

# Chronologies

Most of the unfolding events of Barney's accident and what happened in the following weeks and months, I learned much later on. I have to acknowledge my lack of awareness of the detail of his purgatory at the time. And the detail is what matters. You don't have to take so much notice of suffering if you don't see the detail. It's just a word. It has to be broken down into its moments, the generalities scraped away.

I had already booked flights to Europe and within a week was walking from France into Spain, not oblivious, but with no real idea of his moment-by-moment struggle. I hadn't gone up to visit him before I left. I had work, a class to teach, and I had thought there wasn't enough time to get to the hospital in Brisbane and back in the few days I had left.

It seems brutal to even mention my own walking alongside this moment. What am I doing putting my hundreds of kilometres of trekking in the same cartography as his few metres of agony? They don't overlap, they are not even parallel. Nor are our time streams measurable by the same clocks; suffering and pleasure run in different chronologies. His story is stalled in unbearable moments, mine is in weeks and years.

And yet we have found ourselves meeting in our stories for the first time. As I walked the old paths of Europe I thought about family, how more and more central it becomes in the labyrinth of memory: I thought about my brothers and sisters, my mother who had died a year ago, but especially I thought about Barney. I imagined him flying, swooping elegantly through the sky, and then, in a few horrifying seconds, hurtling feet first towards to the too-solid earth. It's a moment that doesn't bear imagining in too much detail and yet I kept returning to it; the moment he hit the ground, believing he would either die or never walk again.

I thought of him, still think of him, lying on his back in the paddock, wondering if he was dead. And then knowing he wasn't. One moment life was the same as it always was, and then, a moment later, flesh and bones were mangled and the sun just kept on shining. 'The sun shone / As it had to on the white legs disappearing into the green …'

Flashes of our childhood returned to me, unrelated to anything in the present: a phrase, 'the scent of magnolias', from a ghost story he let us listen to on his transistor radio as we lay out on the parched summer lawn one night; hearing him pluck, note by note, 'The Lion Sleeps Tonight' on his guitar; him deriding me when I said I wanted to read 'the classics', knowing I had no idea what 'the classics' were; me sneaking into his room to read the book about creatures of the deep sea he had hidden under the bed; admiring him and all my brothers in their cricket whites, sleeves rolled up ready to go to town; crying to Mum in the kitchen because he had taunted me, again, about my horrible red hair and freckles; watching him hang over the back of a kitchen chair, tracing with his finger the lino pattern when we were meant to be praying the Rosary. They were random and insignificant scenes, as if my brain was splicing together a video, not of highlights, but the daily life of ordinary squabbling kids.

I keep asking questions, Barney keeps answering. Mostly in writing. I send him the first part of the story I have written and ask him to check the facts. I tell him to allow me some poetic licence, which makes him laugh. He answers with precise detail and generosity, but there is something impermeable about the facts he sends. They are beautiful facts, but I am outside them. Most of the time I have to find a way in, and the only way I can think of is to walk with them.

On the day he sends me sent me his corrections, it's late when I head out. I get up from my writing desk and head out the door towards Woolloomooloo Bay at the end of my street. The sun has gone down, and twilight doesn't last long in Sydney so it will be dark by the time I get back. But I need to go now. I've been thinking about the long years when we didn't see each other, despite a childhood on the farm together. Why do I want to tell his story now? The question is still there.

The cafes on the wharf are noisy with people having dinner, but as soon as I head up the stone steps to the gardens, it is quiet. I gaze at peppermint gums, blackbutt, scribbly gums, apple gums, paperbarks, grevillea, bottlebrush, Moreton Bay figs. And at the sandstone, wind-carved with lacy patterns. The patterns have been here for eons, slowly changing. I am merely a shadow passing by them, a faint vibration.

I'm trying to understand, too, why walking has such a hold over me, why it exerts such an irresistible pull. And I know it's not just me, there's hundreds of thousands of us tramping over the earth like a nomadic tribe that never stays in one place for more than a night. Day-after-day walking, where each morning we get up merely to walk. When we are walking, our whole life happens; when we are not walking, we dream and plan the next long walk. Does it have any purpose, let alone meaning? It needs to be faced before I go too much further.

It's not all blasts of joy on wild fells; in fact, it rarely is. Although I've never weighed it up, on balance there must be more pain, irritation, fear, anger, hunger, blisters, rain, sweat, bruises and the need to pee when there's no tree or rock to squat behind. And yet I don't want to even consider not walking.

It's not as if I've seen everything already. I've not travelled much of the world at all; I've not seen vast tracts of my homeland, Australia; I've never been to North or South America, Africa, Russia, the Middle East, most of Asia, half of Europe. At a walking pace, I'm not likely to see much of it either, even if I walked, as I'd like to, for the rest of my life. It seems impractical and pointless and then there's the secret worry that it's self-indulgent, and yet I can't shake off the desire.

I don't have to walk; I'm not impelled to trudge with animals in the hot sun in search of fresh grasses, nor plod all the way to the well and back to get water for the village. I don't have to stumble thin-bodied to a food depot to save my skeleton children from death, nor flee on foot with millions of others from chemical weapons and bombs falling on my home. I walk for hundreds of kilometres across plains and mountains, scramble down rocky slopes, trudge through snow, ford streams, because I choose to, because I'm trying to find … God knows what? That pulls me up in my tracks, but only briefly. The longing is still there.

# The JOY of HIGH PLACES

At school, I listened to the stories of Aborigines who went walkabout, as it was called, to find new sources of food and water or to visit sacred sites. I lived in the same place on the farm – on Wiradjuri country, without knowing it – day after day, year after year and the only elsewhere was in books. The idea of walking to somewhere else and then back, a rhythmic departure and return, promised the excitement of difference and the reassurance of home. You never knew what you might find in a new place: caves in hillsides, gold in rivers, baby kangaroos, bones of prehistoric dinosaurs.

At high school there were the stories of hundreds of thousands people walking across Europe during and after both world wars, escaping their bombed-out homes. There were gaunt prisoners of war being marched across Germany to Eastern Europe, partisans flitting like shadows through forests and along hedgerows. And black and white images of families on exposed roads, mothers holding babies and carrying suitcases, children struggling along behind, which meant that walking was also brave and heroic. It was not for the faint-hearted.

Walking was also claimed by the philosophers. Aristotle founded the Peripatetic school of philosophy around 300 BC. He and his students walked about the Lyceum, their school in Athens, as they aired and questioned their thoughts. Peripatetic, in fact, means *given to walking*. I like that phrase, the sense of walking being something that you willingly offer yourself to, that you allow to possess you.

I am *given* to walking.

I went to Athens not so long ago, on my way back from a walk in Crete, and trudged across town, still in my walking boots, to see the ruins of the Lyceum. It had lain under other buildings for centuries and was only rediscovered and opened to the public in 2009. Although the Parthenon and the museums were packed with tourists, there was only one other person at the Lyceum. I wandered around the low walls and bare lines of bricks, aware of putting my feet in Aristotle's footsteps.

Contemporary science reveals walking is good for your health, just in case I hadn't noticed. Walking improves brain function and sense of wellbeing, and not just because of the calming effect of moving at a natural pace through the world. Data suggests there is a relationship between footfall and blood flow, the impact of the foot hitting the ground creating pressure waves, which force an increase in blood flow to the brain. Apparently there is an optimising rhythm between brain blood flow and walking, as if walking is tuning the brain.

All this mythology and history, philosophy and science could be seen as a defence against accusations of time-wasting, a sensitivity to the fact that not everyone can wander at length across the planet. I could try to argue that I walk simply and frugally, but there is no getting around the reality that I can do it because I'm a western woman with enough time on her hands.

All I can do is trace my walks in, one by one, to see what can be made of them. I have been on long distance walks every year since Barney's fall. The chronology of the walks doesn't matter that much, but the one from France over the Pyrénées was nearest in time to Barney's fall and his excruciating shuffle back from the abyss. I straighten the map, which is already a bit tattered, and start marking in the route.

# A handful of people

*St-Jean-Pied-de-Port, France to Logroño, Spain*

On the first day of walking across the Pyrénées, I thought walking was about physical effort. It was only a couple of hours since I had started and I was already feeling stretched on the first slope. Ridges and peaks rolled away to the horizon on either side of me, looking at this angle, like the spines of some vast green creature. The air was quiet and still. I stopped to listen to the silence and heard crickets, bees, flies, cowbells.

It was mid-afternoon, the hottest time of the day, and with the unaccustomed steep climb I was overheated and sweaty. My genetically Irish complexion flushed with sun and exertion and I was suddenly light-headed and nauseous. My arms felt bulky and I looked down to see that my hands were swollen, with blotchy white and red fingers. My heart beat faster and I felt faint.

'I feel weird,' I said. 'I think I might have heat-stroke or something.'

I sat down on a rock on the side of the path and asked Anthony to look in the guidebook. I sounded calm but felt panicked. What if I wasn't up to crossing mountains and walking hundreds of kilometres. In real time, it was my first long-distance walk. What if I keeled over and fell off the edge of a cliff, smashed like Barney. What if all of us were being picked off now that our mother was gone. My mind was over-colouring the scene and wouldn't stop.

'Sit down. Sips of water,' Anthony read. 'Wait until you cool down before you walk again. If it's heat-exhaustion, stay cool and have some water; if it's heat-stroke, stay cool and get medical help, it could be fatal.'

'That's not what it says.'

'It does. Are you dizzy? Restless?'

'What? No. I'm hot and my hands are swollen and I feel sick.'

'So it's heat exhaustion. And probably dehydration. You'll be right.'

After sitting for 40 minutes cooling down and sipping water I stood again, ready to keep walking. It was still hot and I overheated again quickly, which forced me to stop every 100 metres or so to sip more water. By the time I arrived at the refuge at Orisson, under ten kilometres away but a 600-metre gain in altitude, I felt as if I'd been walking all day.

At the refuge, Anthony and I were allocated bunk beds in a dormitory and that night shared in the group meal. After dinner, each person was asked to say where they were from and why they were walking.

'Australia,' I said. 'And I don't know why.' I didn't even think about my brother.

# The JOY of HIGH PLACES

Next morning in the Pyrénées, Anthony and I were on the road before dawn. It was cold and shadowy, the dark silhouettes of mountain spines – perhaps a vast sleeping dragon – stretched out around us in the dreamscape. The cool air and the altitude created a sense of being in the sky and I remembered dream-flying in the night air as a child. Even in the dim light I could see forever, like an eagle circling above the wild terrain. I was reminded of my brother flying and for a moment knew that he must have turned into a bird, wing above his head, floating and circling, looking down on the far world. The full 360 degrees shape of hills and valleys revealed in his binocular eagle-vision, must have been what drew him in, caught him. What would he do now? Even if he did manage to walk properly again, it surely would not be enough for him.

Gradually the dark shapes of fence posts and fields and ridges began to fill with colour: distinct emerald blades of grasses, and leaves of marshmallow and mint and yarrow by the side of the road, and further away a smooth dense green cloaking the slopes which turned blue at the horizon. Then the sky was a brilliant fiery red against the blue and velvety green, creating a drama of light and shadow in the folds of ridges and glittering on a multitude of dewdrops, an absurd display of heart-cracking beauty.

I kept craning my neck to the east, awestruck. I should have been silenced by the beauty, but the landscape was so new to my mind that it couldn't help trying to name everything: the glowing light, the dragon spine ridges, the fiery sun.

The road became a wide, grassy path, steep and zigzagging further up, high above the clouds into the wild mountains. On the slopes there were shaggy, black-legged sheep with bells, woolly ponies, and occasional shepherds in four-wheel drives. It was the country of the Basque shepherds, traditionally keepers of sheep in the high country, a people who have their own words for everything.

A cattle grid indicated the border into Spain, and on the other side was a sign in both Spanish and Euskara, the Basque language. Basque isn't related to any other Indo-European language, the language tree that most European and many Indian languages branched from, although to my uneducated ear, there was an Eastern European sound to the conglomeration of g's and z's, x's and k's. There's a genetic continuity between present-day Basques and their Palaeolithic ancestors, which means they have been in this country just about as long as the Wiradjuri have been in theirs. And they already had their own language when Indo-Europeans arrived. My heritage is of transplantation, so I cannot know what effect tens of thousands of years in the same country and the same language would have on genetic memory.

'Kaixo,' I said to myself. Hallo.

'Zer Meduz?' How are you?

'Egun ona izan dezazalu.' Have a nice day.

The words clicked under my tongue, softly.

The path continued to climb. My feet and legs felt strong now, the sun was warm. 'On top of the world,' I thought. The first day was an aberration. I could do this. Anthony, ahead of me, turned around and smiled as if I had said it aloud.

That evening in the monastery at Roncesvalles, I met James for the first time. He was sitting across the table, a stocky, dark-haired Australian, listening and watching. I felt drawn to him, even before he said anything. I recognised a combination of traits

I've always found intriguing: a sweetness of nature paired with concealed hurt. I think he said he came from northern New South Wales, but I'm not sure about that. What I do remember is a shadowing in his eyes and a sense that his sweetness had been wounded. Somehow his well-being mattered to me immediately, but I was also curious about the shadow.

He was sitting beside Anthony and they talked for a while. I found myself leaning in, trying to catch their conversation. Afterwards Anthony and I returned to our small cubicle in the dormitory but neither of us mentioned James.

We arranged our packs around two Austrian boys who were sharing the cubicle with us. One of them had a carved wooden walking stick, a *stocknagel*, which his grandfather had carried with him all over the Austrian Alps when he was a young man, 50 years earlier. It was a dark-coloured wood and had tin mementoes from his grandfather's journeys nailed onto it. I saw the Austrian several more times along the road in the next several days; he became 'the boy who was taking his grandfather's stick on another walk'.

In the morning, the *hospitalière* at the monastery woke everyone by walking along the corridors chanting 'Alleluia'. Apart from the yearning sound of the call to prayer in Istanbul, it was the most soothing way to be called into the waking world I have ever experienced. I thought of Montaigne, the sixteenth-century French essayist, who, when he was a child, was woken every morning by the strains of a harpsichord; his father believed that no-one should be dragged harshly into consciousness. For me as a child, it was the magpies and the kookaburras I listened to as I awoke. I realised for the first time that Barney must have listened to the same sounds, but we had never talked about it, never elaborated our shared library of sense memories. The 'Alleluia' echoed down the corridor, diminishing in volume and then increasing as the singer walked back up past the reluctant bodies.

Out in the cool air before dawn, the path led through a beech forest. The leafy covering made it even darker, so that I had to use my torch. Other walkers passed by, dim shadows in the gloom. I had my first pang of the pointlessness of it; walking through the dark just to get to the next town. I was floating, untied from my moorings, bobbing on some wide dark ocean. I suddenly knew that although I was long grown-up, I was slightly adrift without my mother there in the background. I caught up and walked beside Anthony for several steps.

'It's an odd thing to be doing,' I said. 'Walking across a foreign country before the sun is up. It doesn't make sense, really.'

'Nor do most things,' he said.

Anthony touched shoulders with me and our packs bumped together. Putting words to it were enough to reattach the solid world. My mother was gone, my brother had fallen from the sky, but we wouldn't all fall apart. I settled, re-knotted myself and walked on, watching out for tree roots and sticks in the torchlight, reassured by the yellow arrows painted on posts and trees and rocks. The limits of the path formed a line through the vast unknown. For this time, in these terms of reference, I could find my way.

Soon there were meadows, and beech forests now dappled with light, an oak wood on the side of a hill, and then pine forest, fresh smelling and carpeted with pine needles. In the meadows there were more black-legged sheep, short shaggy horses and golden cows. Each tree and animal carried an aura of the imaginary made real, a sense that by some powerful magic, they had come into being. They were now existing, but still shimmered with their recent magical translation into the physical world.

I walked easily for most of the day, but by afternoon, one toe was starting to feel sore. When I took my boot off and examined it, I realised the toe was naturally bent under and the all-day walking was causing it to be squashed by the other toes. It hurt but it didn't seem to be anything to worry about.

We stopped at a village and bought cheese, apples and a bread stick for lunch, then sat in a soft green field and ate. We didn't carry much food because our packs were small, the size of other people's day-packs, with just the essentials of a change of clothes, raincoat, toiletries, compass, thermos, thin towel and sheet bag. Villages were mostly five or six kilometres apart, and because it was such a well-walked pilgrimage route, there was always a cafe to buy a tortilla and *jambon* so there was no need to carry supplies. Some of the way was in the wilds, over mountains and through woods, but I realised that I liked the feeling of walking through a landscape that had been long-settled, vineyards and fig trees offering ripe fruit, and of walking into a medieval village where there was sure to be a quiet square and a shot of coffee.

That evening in Zubiri, Anthony and I saw James in a bar. We sat down at a table and he came to sit with us as if it had been arranged. I noticed my delight and felt disconcerted. It wasn't a physical attraction, perhaps motherly – he looked the same age as one of my sons. We drank beer and talked but I have no recall of what we said to each other although I can picture where we sat, the veneer table and the computers in the dim light at the back of the bar. The pain in him was evident in the shadowing of his eyes but he made no mention of it.

# A handful of people

'There's something about him,' Anthony said later.
'You too?' I said.

On the way to Pamplona next day, I started listing the people I had met: the Austrian boy, James, an older French man who loved Arabic culture, a Japanese couple, a middle-aged Frenchwoman and her 20-year-old son who kept losing each other, a Canadian surfie with tangled blond hair. It was a way of distracting myself from my toe, which had become painful, much more painful than seemed reasonable to expect from one squashed small toe. I pulled my boot off to examine it again and it was white and shapeless, looking like a flattened haricot bean.

The track, now sandy dirt, crossed the Rio Argo twice and headed under a major road through a dirty tunnel and across a Romanesque bridge. I made an effort to appreciate the stone curve of the bridge before I hobbled over it. Now my shin was sore as well and the pain in my toe had sharpened and filled my brain. When I checked it again it was now blistered as well as squashed, and almost unrecognisable as a toe. The toenail had disappeared and the flesh was moist like a slug. I tried to wrap more blister pads around it but they squashed the toe further. It was pitiful that one small appendage could have taken over my experience. Anger, and then shame, flickered through my mind. I had no right to even mention it when my brother was still in hospital.

I saw a doctor in Pamplona who explained that my toe was deformed – he couldn't tell whether naturally or from shoes that were too small when I was a child – and that long walking simply squashed it. He thought there was little to be done except to stop walking. I re-bandaged it and kept going.

# The JOY of HIGH PLACES

The landscape on the other side of Pamplona was dry with stripped autumn wheatfields and vineyards. A concave hillside of stripped wheat lifted my heart and I gazed at it hungrily, a hillside from childhood, the same blue of sky behind it, the same warmth in the air. The slope and curve aroused not a memory, but a sensation of unquestioning reassurance.

After 25 kilometres we stopped in the small medieval town of Puente La Reina where there was a church founded in the twelfth century by the Knights Templar. I decided to go to Mass that evening, remembering sitting in the church in Wellington; the marble altar and painted statues, the gold-embroidered vestments, the enveloping dimness. In those days I'd sat with my brothers and sisters, my mother and father, each of us in our best clothes and shiny shoes, trying to believe. Then I remembered my mother not bothering to go to church any more during the last few years of her life. At first I thought it was because it was too far for her to walk, but then even when I visited with my car, she didn't accept the offer of a lift down to the church. I wondered if she had stopped believing but it wasn't the sort of question to ask aloud. Did she think of Barney refusing to go to church all those years ago? She told me once that Dad had felt shame about hitting Barney that time. Not just that he had lost his temper and hit his son, but that he had caused Barney to lose 'the Faith'. I told her Barney was never going to be a believer. 'That's what I told him,' my mother had said.

That evening at Puente La Reina I listened to the Mass in Spanish, recognising the rhythm of the words, the shape of the ritual, the round white bread that everyone appeared to accept was the actual flesh and blood of God the Son. Women the age my mother had been when she died sat in black dresses in the candlelight. I had given up belief a long time ago, but I liked the incense, the robes and chanting, the light glittering on the excess of gilt.

The next morning the path led out through the silence of the medieval town, with only the sound of boots on cobbles and the feel of cool air on skin. As I crossed the eleventh-century bridge on the edge of town I looked up and saw Orion's Belt in the south-east and Venus low in the sky. Behind us red rays fanned out through pure gold clouds.

In the cool of the morning when the vineyards were deserted, I took a bunch of black grapes from the end of a row and they tasted as cool as the morning. By the time the sun was well up, there were pickers and large baskets full of shiny grapes at the ends of rows and more baskets stacked on a trailer attached to a tractor. I saw an old fig tree and hummed a song I had learned a few years before: 'Everyone 'neath their vine and fig tree, shall live in peace and unafraid.' For a few hours my feet didn't trouble me and all was well in the world.

The country we were passing through was drier still, clods of earth crumbling underfoot, wheat stubble in fields, ancient almond trees in a field above the path, stone walls holding the path on either side. The almonds, their thick, greying coats splitting, hung within arm's reach and I picked handfuls and put them in my pocket.

'I spent summers in the almond trees when I was a kid,' I said, by way of justification. 'On the farm.'

I could see my brothers, Barney, Tim and Kevin, and sister Mary, skinny legged, perched in the trees, eating as many almonds as we could – peeling, cracking and biting – in between filling a bucket to bring back to the house for everyone else.

I remembered my mother saying every spring, 'Aren't the almond trees the most beautiful thing you have ever seen?' One year, when I was 12, I looked at the drift of pink and white – there were five almond trees – and realised that they *were* beautiful, and that beauty was to be remarked on. Years later I was reminded of this when I was driving with my teenage son under a stand of maples in their autumn fire – red, cerise, pink – along a street we had driven along many times before.

'Has it always been like this?' he asked in astonishment.

There must be a moment in each life when we suddenly become conscious of beauty for the first time – and then the need to paint, or write, or sing it. I thought of Barney's painting, his determination to pin down an almost photographic record of the world. Years ago he had made a painting of Dad walking across the farm, with Baron Rock behind him, the wheat shed and chooks, and Dad's felt hat – clear and detailed – and had given it to him. It seemed to be a peace offering.

I squatted and cracked open the almonds with a rock. They were very hard, I suppose from the dry weather, and not as sweet as the almonds of childhood.

The track led over a Roman bridge, and the road – once cambered, with stones set lengthwise in the middle – continued over the dry hills. The 2000-year-old surface, now pocked and irregular and often sharp, made my feet slip and my ankles turned alarmingly. The squashing pain had returned. I diverted my thoughts away from it, giving myself particular events from long ago to remember in detail: the autumn day I walked across the paddocks towards the farmhouse when I was a teenager; it was stormy and windy, spitting rain, and the proud exhilaration of wild weather filled my body. The bloody toe – it was bloody by now – intruded in the spaces between memory.

The last two hours to the next town, La Estrella, stretched. I hobbled behind Anthony, thinking several times I would have to stop, but each time knowing I wouldn't. I didn't have a clear idea why I had to go on; perhaps it was the conviction that walking had become a metaphor for what was happening to Barney. I don't think I clearly articulated it to myself at the time, but there was a sense that giving up wasn't an option. I don't believe it's necessary to suffer to be transformed, but it felt laughable to be defeated by a literally bloody toe when Barney was struggling to find a way to live inside a mangled body.

As we sat in a courtyard in La Estrella drinking beer, James walked in and joined us. We exchanged the usual 'How are your feet, and where did you start from this morning, and is there somewhere good to eat here?' I bided my time to ask what I really wanted to know.

'Why are you walking?' I asked it casually enough, just another usual question.

'I finished my degree and didn't know what to do next. I just decided to walk. You know, for something to do. Things to get away from. What about you?'

'I don't know really. We both just wanted to walk. I'm hoping I'll find out. What are you getting away from?'

'The usual. Whatever.' He looked uncomfortable. I'd been too quick and obvious. 'Why, do I need to have a big reason?'

'No. I don't have one either,' I said. 'I just think there is one with you. I can see it, something difficult, I just don't know what it is.'

He looked caught out, but he covered and shrugged. 'I'll just keep that to myself, thanks.'

I had the sense to shut up at last. He and Anthony talked for a while, the easy talk of men who like and respect each other, both of them with a better sense of the right distance to keep than I had.

On the last day, we walked out again through the quiet dark. I have a photograph of that morning in La Estrella, the golden glow of a streetlamp on the wall opposite me as I pass along the stone alleyway, alone except for the unseen photographer. I seem to have an easy gait at that early hour.

The path led up through a dense forest of gnarled trees whose name I don't know. The forest had a feeling that it had been here forever and would be here forever, long past the time any humans might pass through it. Its dispassionate age was unnerving. It was tough, much tougher than me and it would give me nothing because I was irrelevant to its existence. I was glad to enter into a sweet-smelling pine forest, soft needles underfoot, clear of undergrowth, a sense of space and greenish light.

Anthony stopped by the path in the pines to take a photograph of whorls of clouds in the western sky, pink from the reflected glory of the sunrise which itself was not visible. While we were stopped James appeared on the path behind us. I again had the strong, almost overwhelming feeling of wanting to connect. It was uncanny, so apparently irrational, although later when I confessed it again to Anthony, he again said he felt the same. In that moment in the forest, I was suddenly unsure. I had stepped over a mark the previous night.

He smiled as he approached, but I could see his uncertainty.

'Are you stalking us?' I said as he reached speaking distance. I said it lightly but there was some rejection in the words and my body was turned away towards the reflected sunrise. I wanted him to stop but didn't want him to know I wanted it. He slowed down, almost stopped, made some remark in return, and kept walking. I felt a pang of guilt. I had done the wrong thing.

I remembered my mother telling me a story about how she had once seen a tough-looking young woman struggling with a pram on the stairs of a railway station. She had spiky hair, Mum said. And tattoos. Mum wanted to help her, but she thought the young woman might tell her to clear out and mind her own business.

'I didn't help her,' my mother said. 'Just because I was scared of being told off.'

I thought of all the times I hadn't helped someone in the street. 'We all do the wrong thing sometimes,' I said.

Then the path was back into dense, ancient woods; a closed-in, almost claustrophobic air. The trees were not tall, but crowding, tangled and dim, grey-trunked, twisted. There was something fear-inducing about them, unwelcoming.

It was mid-afternoon when we reached Los Arcos, a town built in the middle ages with a central square and arched doorways through the city wall. I slipped off my pack and sat down at one of the tables in the square. It was the end of the walk, but I knew that something had entered my soul, that this was by no means the end of it.

Some walkers had arrived before us and others were still arriving. I saw the young Austrian with his grandfather's stick, and the French mother and son. The sun was shining in a cloudless sky and the square was half in bright light, half in deep shade, like a chiaroscuro painting, profoundly dramatic. Nothing dappled, nothing in-between – not like life, I thought. Some people were staying the night in Los Arcos; a few, like us, were finished, catching the bus to somewhere else. Our destination had been Logroño, only 27 kilometres away, but we had run out of time to walk it.

I took my boots off, and sat in my bare feet, letting the sweat dry. The toe still looked a mess, but it had not defeated me. There was some pride in that; not enough to say it aloud, or even think of comparing it to Barney's long-lasting agony, but there was a flicker of satisfaction.

I looked up and saw James sitting at another table several metres away in the deep shadow. I hadn't seen him arrive; he must have come from the other side of the square.

'He looks like he's staying here. We should say goodbye,' I said. But I didn't get up.

'Let's finish our drinks,' said Anthony.

I stretched out my legs, put my arms behind my head, closed my eyes against the sun. There was plenty of time in the slowed down middle of the afternoon. The minutes stretched and bent. I could feel in my nerve ends what I should do. Then James got up, shrugged on his backpack and walked through the chairs and tables into the bright sunlight and left the square through the stone archway. It was the last time either of us saw him.

That was five years ago and I still often wonder what happened to James. I don't mean what happened on the walk. I knew he was heading for Santiago de Compostela, the end of the pilgrims' route, and would have made it. I mean what happened to him to make the shadow in his eyes. Sometimes questions are not answered, connections are not made.

# Lucy

What happened to Barney next? That's always the question, the unbreakable thread tying each moment to the next. What happens next? After the accident, it was a continuous unfolding – at least to the rest of us, his family and flying friends. To Barney it was an unrelenting present of pain and drugged confusion. I had rung Jenny before I'd left to go walking. All of us rang, his brothers and sisters, his adult children. Jenny was reassuring, practical, tired. This was days later. We rang each other, trying to find out without burdening her or Barney with our anxieties.

'I don't think I can get up there to see him,' I said.

'Don't feel guilty,' Kathy said. Two of our older brothers, Peter and Kevin, who both lived up that way, would see him as soon as possible.

I rang Barney at the hospital before I caught my flight.

'What's the story?' I said.

'I'll tell you one day,' he said. He sounded unendurably weary.

# The JOY of HIGH PLACES

What happened next – the list of emailed questions, for the first day:

Did you sleep the night of the operation? (or was your brain speeding over everything all night?)

What was your room like? Colour? Did it have a view?

Were you alone or were there other patients?

What was the weather like? Sunny? Rainy?

When you first woke, did you remember instantly what had happened or did you wonder where the hell you were?

How does a person feel after anaesthetic?

How did you feel – physically? Emotionally?

Could you eat? What food did they give you? Or did you have a feeding tube?

Were you attached to various machines or drips?

Were you wearing one of those blue or green gowns that tie up at the back?

Was Jenny back on that day? How was she? (She can answer that one if she wants!!)

Did the surgeon come to see you? (He or she? I won't use their name; I just want to picture them.)

Did anyone else come and see you?

Could you talk or did you just want everyone to leave you alone?

Are there any particular nurses or anyone else you remember from that day? Your attention to everything, I imagine, was very heightened?

You said you were on a cocktail of drugs – what were they exactly?

# Lucy

When Barney woke the morning after the accident in Princess Alexandra hospital, the sun was shining. He could see blue sky out the window. He could see! He felt a flood of relief and joy. In all the trauma and shock, his mind had latched onto the possibility of losing his sight as its first priority. The wide blue sky embraced him, welcomed him back.

But then he became aware of his body. He was lying on his back with pillows under both his arms and under his lower legs. He only knew that by peering under the sheet. He could not feel his legs. He tried to move his right foot. There was a blank as if the impulse had hit a wall of cotton wool. He tried the other foot. Nothing. The same weird nothing. He felt sick. He was wearing a blue hospital gown made of paper – he remembered his clothes being cut off him the day before – and there were tubes coming from his body to machines and drip bags: monitoring electrodes, multiple cannulas in both arms attached to drips, a catheter attached to a bag threaded into his bladder, a tube into his back to drain blood from his spine, and a tube for an opioid with a trigger button which he learned he could operate himself for the pain.

For the pain.

It was all-enveloping. There was burning pain, aching, freezing, throbbing pain. The pain of bruised and battered internal organs, broken bones, the surgeon's knife, and the peculiar distress of nerve pain. And nausea. He wanted to vomit. Dread surged through him. A black wave of despair. He said much later that he wished then, and many times afterwards, that he had been killed outright. He remembered the plummet towards earth and the sight of green, soft-looking grass, those few moments which could have been his last. That would have been better.

But there were people around his bed. He recognised the surgeon, Chinese he thought, and other doctors and nurses. Were they the operating team? His head felt weirdly clear, but he couldn't remember. The surgeon asked him if he knew what had happened to him. Barney said yes, he'd had a paragliding crash and broken his back.

The surgeon said the operation had been a success. He had been able to do what he set out to do. But that didn't mean he was making any promises about walking again.

'You have suffered significant spinal nerve damage. I couldn't reverse that, no-one could, I could only prevent it from getting worse. The extent of your recovery depends on how well your body can repair itself. That's individual, it depends on your inheritance and general health.'

Barney felt a small surge of hope. He was fit and healthy from flying and from dancing – he and Jenny went to dance classes a couple of times a week – he hadn't smoked cigarettes or drunk alcohol since he was a teenager, he had a healthy diet.

'No promises, but maybe with a year or so of rehab, if you work hard at it, you may be able to walk with the aid of crutches.'

The pain and nausea made it hard to concentrate. Someone explained about the opioid trigger. That he could press it whenever the pain was unbearable. He pressed it. Within a few seconds he felt a warm rush through his veins. He had never felt anything like it before. The pale grey wall behind the doctors and nurses rippled upwards. They melted away and then there was no-one there. He looked around. He was in a smallish room, a recovery room, he realised later when he was moved, either later that day or the next day, into a two-bed ward.

# Lucy

He was aware of someone else in the room, was it before or after he was moved? Another patient, a young man, injured in a car accident he learned later. Then he disappeared and there was someone else in the bed. What happened to him; did he recover or die? Was he walking around somewhere with the memory of a middle-aged man smashed up from a paragliding accident sometimes flitting through his head?

Jenny rang in the morning. He had rung her the night before, just minutes before the operation. She had been shopping in Rundle Mall in Adelaide, buying a few items for her father – new pyjamas? slippers? – and answered in her usual pragmatic style. She was as practical and sensible as Barney – extreme events did not happen in their lives – and it took more than a few beats for it to sink in. And then he had to go, the surgeon was waiting, and she was left standing in the Mall, her life at right angles to the moment before she answered her phone.

She had been with Barney since they were in their early twenties. They were both teachers and they'd had three children together, but perhaps more than most couples, they lived for each other. They didn't socialise much, spent most of their spare time together, playing golf, dancing, or simply being at home sharing their evenings and weekends, Barney painting exact scenes, Jenny looking up exotic meals to cook. When Barney took up flying it had been a bit worrying, but she supported his dream, there was no question she would do otherwise.

'How are you?' The same question as the surgeon, as everyone, but from Jenny it was a lifeline. She was someone who needed him to be okay. He answered with all the positives. He was alive. There was hope he could walk with crutches in a year or so. There was a brilliant team looking after him. Jenny told him she had arranged a flight back and would see him tomorrow. It was the best she could do.

Barney said it was hard to remember the details of the first day, what happened when. The days melted together. The opioids dissolved events and the walls. There was Oxycontin and another one was called Endone – a strangely threatening name for a dreamy drug. He remembers sleeping, waking up with pain, eating meals that were hard to keep down – perhaps nausea from the after-effects of the anaesthesia – or perhaps his traumatised stomach and bowels just could not deal with it. He did remember the meals were 'edible, but not entertaining'.

Nurses came in and out giving him an endless array of drugs, Tramadol, Paracetamol, Gabapentin, Norfloxacin, Motilium, Lactulose, Docusate, and the Oxycontin and Endone. Not that he knew what any of them were at that stage.

Perhaps Drew or Jason, who had first swooped down to help him, arrived briefly, or perhaps that was the next day. Perhaps Kevin, the fourth of the five brothers in our family, came too, or perhaps the next day. Barney didn't remember any phone calls but he might have talked to me. To Kathy. Or Mary. He slept on and off all day.

There seemed to be creatures – monkeys were they? – and mechanical objects, perhaps made of Lego, crawling on the walls, but nothing seemed definitely itself, more like they were melting from one thing to another, like a Salvador Dali painting. When he asked about the rippling walls and the creatures, the nurses told him he was hallucinating. He remembered Dad exclaiming about the little creatures at the end of his bed before he died, and Mum remarking on the little dog and the kangaroo in her hospital room in the weeks before her death.

He did recall that a male nurse and a physiotherapist arrived with a contraption called a 'rollator'. It was a high frame on steel rollers with metal curved armrests on either side, like two small troughs – and apparently he was meant to stand in the frame and try walking.

'We think you can give it a go. What do you reckon?' said the nurse. It was more an instruction than a question.

It wasn't possible. If he couldn't move his feet or lower legs in the bed, couldn't even sense where his legs were, how could he stand, let alone move? And there were all the tubes and bags he was attached to.

Barney nodded. What else could he do?

They pushed his trolley table out of the way and parked the rollator next to his bed, and then the nurse pushed a button to elevate the head-end of the bed so that he was sitting straight up. Everything hurt, searing absurd pain.

The drip stand was arranged next to the rollator, then together, the nurse and physiotherapist folded down his sheet and cotton cell blanket. Then they lifted him expertly out of the bed and into the frame, both of them holding his weight the whole time. Then they put his arms along the troughs so that he could support his own weight with his forearms. They continued to hold him, their arms linked around his, one of them carrying his urine bag and the other reaching for the drip stand. Now they were a procession, ready to begin.

'Just slide your feet,' said the physiotherapist. Her voice was warm and encouraging. Barney looked down. He could see his swollen feet in white compression socks on the pale green vinyl floor, but he couldn't feel the surface. There was none of the familiar pressure of floor beneath feet, so familiar that he had never noticed it was there before. Perhaps he had been aware of it when he was a baby first learning to walk on the lino floor of the farmhouse, the undulating feel of his foot muscles trying to find balance, his bare soles sensing the firmness, the reliability under his unsteady chubby legs. But of course he had forgotten that, like we all do, in decades of walking without thought.

I watched my own two boys and, decades later, their own boy and girl, learn to walk, and each time I was struck by the focused determination of the baby to do this very risky thing – standing two-legged, when four-legged is so safe and easy – and by the pleasure everyone who is watching takes in the smallest bipedal step. The baby pulls herself up on chairs and other peoples' legs, keeps a hand on the surface, looks pleased with herself, reaches out to the next available handhold, judges the distance, only takes a step once the new handhold is secured. Feet wobble, muscles adjust; shifting, understanding the surface, gaining strength, comprehending the new concept of balance. And then there is the triumphant moment when she lets go of every handhold and bravely steps out across the empty space to a waiting, smiling parent.

Teetering, focused, glowing with a sense of achievement – what makes her do it? Is it seeing all of us so tall and mobile and powerful, able to move wherever we please? Or is it programmed into her – she would walk even if she were raised by wolves? Feral children, the very few who have lived, have been reported as walking on all fours, so it seems the baby is mimicking our standing and walking. Still, she teaches herself how to do it; she doesn't see adults hauling themselves up on sofas and stepping precariously between furniture. She watches and purposefully teaches herself.

Later, as I bombarded Barney with questions, he said he realised, not right away, but later, that was what he had to do. He had to watch people walking and see how it was done.

'My legs and feet just more-or-less dangled,' he told me. He tried to imagine a step. Even imagining was too hard. His brain felt crystal clear, opioid clear, but he'd never had to imagine a step before. What did a step look like? It didn't matter. No nerve messages were getting through to his feet. A cacophony of nerve messages came from his body to his brain, all carrying notes of pain. But the nurse and physio persisted, gradually rolling him along to the door and back. The grey walls rippled upwards. His feet slid and slipped on the vinyl for perhaps four metres to the door. And back.

How long had it taken? An age. It couldn't be usefully measured by any units of time. It was simple agony and fruitless effort. They helped him back onto his bed. He was totally exhausted and in unimaginable pain.

'I was overwhelmed by the enormity of what I had to try to do. I thought that might be as good as it got,' he said. The nerve damage was too severe. He might try with huge pain and effort and not get anywhere. What was the point?

I can't, don't want to, imagine such pain. Or such despair. It's not an emotion I know about first hand. I know about restlessness, years of it, urgent and agitated at times, which could be one of the reasons that I walk. I have to let urgency and restlessness go when I walk. I can't be in a hurry. I can't be purposeful or focused on the goal. I can't even think of it as a means of getting from here to there, because if I did, I would see there are much more efficient ways of doing it. But for Barney walking, or learning to walk again, was urgent; it either had to be the focus of all his efforts, or given up altogether. There was no certainty that any of the pain and effort would be worth it. It would be easier to lie still, not make any of this more unbearable than it was.

Still, the next day when the nurses returned with the rollator, he tried again. Once again the nurse and physio helped him out of bed and onto the frame and wheeled his drip stand and catheter, but this time, they did not hold onto him. They stood beside him, urging him to take a step, believing in the impossible. He gazed down at his feet. They were still swollen and bruised, he still could not feel the floor, could not even tell if it was warm or cold. With all his weight supported by his elbows, slowly he slid one foot along, using the weak muscle responses in his upper legs. He had moved on his own – or at least with the help of the rollator! He was sweating with the effort, beads of it on his forehead, as he tried again with the other foot.

It was extraordinarily slow and just as painful as the day before, but he made it the four metres to the door with the nurse and physio at his side, cheering him along. And then, an eon later, he made it back to the bed, each second of it excruciating. He lay on the bed, wondering again if this was as good as it would get. He felt he had made no progress, and the pain was worse, if anything, than the day before. There were no promises and no solid precedents for what might happen – no certainty about whether he would ever be able to walk unaided. It was different for everyone, they said, the infinite varieties of damage to the nerves in the spinal column, the infinite combinations of genetic inheritance, and the unmeasurable patterns of will, endurance and hope in any individual person. It might all depend on the day he took his first step on the farm, the exact strength of the pleasure in mastery imprinted in his cerebral cortex.

Of course, no-one remembers that pride and pleasure. Barney learned to walk long before I was born and there is no-one left to report when and how he began, what day it was, sunny or rainy, that he took his first uncertain, proud steps. I know when I began to walk, because there's written evidence. There's a letter, hand-written in ink, apparently from Barney and my sister Kathy, to my mother, reporting that I had walked a few steps and climbed up onto the lounge when I was 12 months old. I've also been told I was atypical in that I was never four-legged – I didn't crawl. I sat upright, and with a flat pincer movement, slithered along on my bum, perhaps to get a better view of the world, until the day I walked and climbed onto the lounge. My mother was in hospital having another baby, Kevin – hence the letters – so I obviously had to get a move along, but like everyone else I was genetically programmed to walk at a particular time.

Barney's almighty efforts made me wonder about the origins of walking. It is, after all, a defining trait of humans, which means Barney was only obeying his genes. Our ancestor, *Australopithecus afarensis* Lucy, named after 'Lucy in the Sky With Diamonds' – apparently the cool paleoanthropologists who discovered her fossilised bones were listening to the Beatles that night in camp – was clearly a walker, perhaps the first. Donald Johanson and his research team found her in 1974, when she poked her elbow through the dry bed of a gully in Ethiopia more than three million years after she died. They knew right away that Lucy was important. She had a small brain but she also had a broad pelvis and thigh-bones that angled in towards the knees, revealing that she walked.

I went to see Lucy in the Muséum National d'Histoire Naturelle in Paris several years ago and was moved and awed by her small form. She looked like a child, about eight years old. I gazed at her in her glass case – at least I thought I was gazing at her. I've since found out the original Lucy is kept securely in Addis Ababa and that I was gazing solemnly at a cast, but, still, Lucy is impressive. She's evidence of the idea that walking led to brain development and not the other way around. Quite simply, because she walked, the human brain grew. I find that one of the most beautiful ideas in all of our history, that we owe our lovely brain labyrinth to walking on two feet.

By 1.9 million years ago, *Homo erectus* – fully upright and by now larger-brained and longer-legged, her curved spine absorbing the shock of her feet hitting the earth – was striding across the savannah. Her rhythmic stride pumped an optimum blood flow to the brain, which grew larger and more complicated and eventually she gave birth to *Homo sapiens*. We are human because we walked. It means walking is a radical act – it is a literal return to what has made us human. When we walked, our brains grew. In a way, it's as simple as that.

And so we all kept walking. Every slithery fish-like baby, in a few brief months, becomes a walking, speaking autocrat. It's as if each human child, in less than two years enacts the entire origin of the species: from aquatic creature, swimming in a sea of amniotic fluid; to crawling primate in a low-level jungle of furniture and legs; to upright *Homo sapien*, walking, running, speaking, asserting dominion.

I doubt Barney was thinking of any of this, but it was there, forcing him through the pain, day after day. The genetic determination to walk.

# Walking around the mountain

*Mont Blanc – Switzerland, France, Italy*

Barney used to email me – and the rest of his brothers and sisters – links to his track-log so we could see where he had flown, but in those days I mostly didn't bother looking at them. There was always something else to do. I realise now it was his way of trying to show us his bird soul.

I study them today: the one from Mt Tamborine in southern Queensland to Wyaralong, a distance of about 70 kilometres, looks like a white string with knots in it at first. Barney said that he had flown at a height of 7000 feet and that if we clicked on the eye-height button on the right of the log, we would be able to track his flight accurately. As I zoom closer in, I can see the detail of knots untangling into loops, the white line spiralling upwards, round and round like a ball of string unspooling; then it lengthens into a long traverse over the ranges and then circles again in the rising thermals, lengthens again, circles again. The ovals and circles above the mountains look fragile, a fine, scrawled writing on the landscape, inscribing his journey through unseen air

## Walking around the mountain

currents. The shape of the spirals, their urgency and fragility, move me. They convey the danger of floating above the earth using only the moods of the air itself to keep you from falling. There was always danger, nothing was certain, but he wasn't afraid. This, to me, is a mystery. When I walked around Mont Blanc I was afraid. I didn't know how to be courageous in the face of physical danger.

I had read about Mont Blanc, the highest mountain in Europe. Its beauty, its grandeur, its terror. It was a landscape I knew nothing about firsthand, only from myths and films. It straddles the borders of France, Italy and Switzerland, 4810 metres of rock, ice and snow, surrounded by peaks of almost equal height. Anthony and I were not climbers, but there is a path around Mont Blanc – 170 kilometres, never actually on it, but circling it with correct awe. To walk around the Mountain, it's necessary to ascend and descend its seven circling mountains, up and over each of the passes.

I had done the research: the Mont Blanc guidebook warned of storms and of snow patches early in the season. Snow patches? I visualised the occasional crunch of snow under the conquering heroine's hefty boots; the vast and extreme beauty of the Alps displayed in every direction. It's obvious my relationship to the Mountain before I started was a relationship to a postcard, a one-dimensional reality – a postcard mountain with postcard snow. As if beauty came for free.

Anthony and I arrived at Les Houches in the Alps and stayed the first night in a small ski chalet, irises waving out the front, a nest of wood-lined rooms, quiet at this time of year. The owner held out his hand. He had no fingers. Frostbite? I wondered if it was a warning. Over dinner, when I showed him our topographical maps, he tried to indicate the path around the mountain with his finger stubs and I was embarrassed to have to keep clarifying with my own precise finger which path he meant. He took hold of a blue highlighter, holding it between thumb and stubs, and marked the path, and then wrote 'snow' in uncontrolled letters in two places on the map.

'Will there be much?' I asked. I put aside my dinner plate to make room to unfold the map further.

He shrugged. He hadn't been up there this year, but there had been unseasonal late snow at the Croix du Bonhomme. That was where we were heading the day after tomorrow. No need to think about that now. His wife served us *tarte aux mirabelles* made from plums grown in their garden.

After dinner we sat in the twilight of the back garden, Anthony reading James Joyce's *Ulysses* aloud from his phone. Walking and reading have gone together almost from the beginning. Every afternoon or evening after walking, we settled in at a bar or garden of a hostel and Anthony read aloud from whatever book he had downloaded. *Ulysses* had been with us for a while.

The Alps towered, craggy, snow-capped, undeniably magnificent, mirroring every image I'd ever seen of them. *Ulysses* flowed like light on Irish whiskey, glinting and shifting every second. I took a few photos of the magnificence on my phone as I listened to Anthony read.

Next morning the mountains had disappeared, obscured by mist and drizzle. I put on every layer – singlet, long-sleeved top, hoodie, walking pants, rain-jacket – and then boots. Now I was an Amazon, metres tall, striding with long limbs, the planet turning under my heel. The short, middle-aged woman in the mirror was merely a cover for this infinitely powerful being in her seven-league boots.

I stood up, shrugged on my pack, and stepped out into the misty air, ready for the Mountain. I glanced back a few times as we left the chalet to try to fix its romantic image in my mind, but the conscious locking of moments in memory rarely works – it's the random moment that stays.

The weather was too damp for the heart-lifting early morning thrill which usually arrived when I started out. The path was steep, up past ski runs, and my calf muscles, not yet warmed up, felt the strain. The drizzle kept me silent. The hair escaping from my rain-hood turned to rat-tails. I plodded on upwards, the dampness starting to strain my determination to be happy, but soon the sun sparkled on puddles and turned raindrops on boughs into rainbow prisms. I swung along through upland meadows and dappled forest, birds I didn't recognise darted and twittered sweetly. By mid-afternoon we reached Le Ferme de Bon Papa. Cathy, whose grandfather had owned the farm, gave us a room and dried our socks and backpacks in front of her fire upstairs. She told us that when her grandfather had owned the farm, during winter the animals were kept downstairs where we were sleeping.

By the time I'd had breakfast next morning the weather had clouded over. We headed through town, crossed a torrent and then entered a birch wood, following the torrent up the valley. Further up, the cobbled path – it was a Roman road – led steeply upwards through chestnuts, birches, cypresses and larches shivering in the cool air. Out of the woods we stopped by a meadow dancing with wildflowers: yellow, pink, blue, mauve, white; cows with bells; patches of sunlight; and more unknown birds singing. I was in a children's book. Shortly though, the terrain became steeper and rockier and soon pines and larches and meadows were left behind, leaving a bare heath-covered landscape.

We came to the first patch of snow, about 20 metres across, and traversed it easily. There were several more patches, each one bigger than the last, but none of them worrying. Between each patch of snow, wildflowers oddly burst out of the marshy *tourbière* or bog: deep blue bells, creamy edelweiss, little pink stars, yellow arnica and white aconite.

And then there was more snow and patches of dark green *tourbière* crisscrossed with streams. The weather was closing in, mist blotting out the mountains ahead, and the path disappeared, leaving only boot prints and pole pricks in the snow to follow.

A young man passed us coming down and said there was a lot of snow ahead. 'Three hours at least,' he said.

'Can you see the path?'

'There's a lot of snow,' he repeated, as if I hadn't understood.

I realised later that I hadn't understood. I had no context for knowing that 'There is a lot of snow' was shorthand for a whole set of dangers and difficulties anyone who had grown up with snow would immediately foresee.

'But it is still possible to follow footprints?'

He shrugged. 'It is possible now but may not be possible later. There could be rain or more snow.'

Anthony and I looked at each other, but there was no question of stopping. We would never circle the Mountain if we kept stopping at mentions of snow. But soon there was only snow, thick and powdery, covering an upland valley where the prints in front of us were clear but often along multiple tracks heading in various directions. There was no sign of the actual path.

The mists swirled and revealed the Mountain sloping upwards towards the passes, first the Col du Bonhomme, followed by the Col de la Croix du Bonhomme. We discussed the multiple tracks and decided on the most well-trodden path, leading up an incline of perhaps 55 degrees. That angle would be hard work on any slope, but with metres of soft snow, it soon became Sisyphean. Each step upwards sank down almost as far as the previous step; the advance for almighty effort was a few centimetres. I stopped every few steps, exhausted by the effort of getting nowhere.

We trudged on. Step, sink, step, sink, rest. It was a kind of torture to the spirit. My heart was beating too hard, straining. At the top, the mountain flattened out to the Plan des Dames, marked by a large pile of stones in honour of a lone Englishwoman who perished here in a blizzard 200 years ago. I placed a stone on the pile. Snow must have swirled around her, obscuring her path, freezing her to death.

You can easily die up here. The fear was beginning in my stomach but I hadn't acknowledged it yet.

Ahead, I could see the two passes, with a long slope and climb between them. The rain was slushy, halfway to snow, but not heavy. I was exhausted already.

'Can we do this?' Anthony asked.

'I don't know. It's only been half an hour in this snow and I'm already ...' I stopped. I didn't want to be the one to make the decision.

We both looked at the two climbs ahead of us. There were

three small figures struggling up the farthest pass. To my surprise, Anthony said decisively, 'We'll go back. Those people passed us hours ago and they are still climbing that hill. With this rain, their footsteps could disappear and then we'd be stuffed.'

I gathered up my pack and turned down the slope I had just climbed. Descending was difficult; I had to stamp back on my heels into the snow with each step to avoid tumbling down the mountain, but it was a relief not to have to struggle upwards.

We stayed back at Le Ferme de Bon Papa and arranged a ride around the spur of the Mountain to the beginning of the next stage. I sat in the cosiness of the bedroom and wrote lists of new geographic sights: aiguilles, glacier, moraine, torrent, cataract, *col*, peak.

Next morning we were dropped off near Les Chapieux. We crossed a bridge over the Torrent des Glaciers and turned up the zigzag path leading to the pass into Italy. I felt a steely determination to make it, to push on through whatever came along, disallowing the idea that I could be beaten. There was something blind about my attitude, a wilful obliviousness to the realities. Looking back on it, it appears that I had the same stubborn determination as Barney as he tried to learn to walk again, but that's giving me too much credit. His determination was against medical expectation and practice, but it was based on knowledge, the biomechanics of how to walk, whereas mine was a kind of bulldozer determination, not informed by anything.

I walked steadily, pausing to look back over the bright green valley, the scattered farm buildings, and then forward to the rocky snow-shawled mountains. Anthony pointed out a bird of prey, a hawk, circling above the valley. There was startling beauty in every direction, the kind that seems to belong in stories, not daily life. I stopped to take pictures of wildflowers, hoping to identify them later: intense blue campanula, alpine forget-me-not, violets and buttercups, purple crocus flowering straight out of the ground, St John's wort and blue northern dragonhead.

We soon came to snow again. Anthony crossed first and I followed in his footsteps, although his stride was longer than mine and sometimes I had to shuffle my feet to ease into his safe boot-print. I realised that I was doing an instant risk assessment of what would happen if I slipped. At first there were only three categories: getting wet and bruised, having a minor injury, suffering a major injury. It wasn't really a thought process – more a quick flick of the eyes noting angle of slope, iciness of snow, proximity of cliffs and torrents.

We came to a steep snow-covered slope with a circular hole in the snow revealing a torrent. The torrent was visible for a metre or two before disappearing again, plunging in its icy tunnel down the mountain. Metres of snow must have covered the stream when it was frozen, but now that it was running again, the snow vault was falling in. There were two sets of footsteps, which stopped at the edge of the hole. I realised there was a fourth category: if I slipped, it meant certain death. It came into my mind that that was what Barney had faced every time he flew. If something went badly wrong up there, two kilometres above the earth, death was a likely outcome. He had to have known, I might die this time, every time.

I stopped, panic speeding my heart rate. I could slip and fall into the hole, or the snow ceiling of the tunnel could give way under me and I would fall in. Either way, the torrent would sweep my body away in an instant.

Anthony crossed, digging his boots in sideways to create a

few centimetres of flatness on the slope. I followed, digging my poles into the snow and leaning up the slope in an effort not to overbalance. I glanced down at the snow-hole and torrent; my heart thumped. It didn't feel real. It was as if I'd slipped into an action movie, the wrong story, by mistake.

Anthony stood on the other side, watching me. Each step took forever, the space was stretching. I could feel the hollow of my stomach. I finally stepped onto safe ground.

'Are you okay to keep going?' Anthony asked.

'Well, I'm not going back over that.' I walked on ahead for a short while.

The land and the sky were white, with a dark smudge of braided footprints here and there, and sometimes, a drift of pink on the snow, apparently dust from the deserts of Egypt. It was a world I didn't know. I looked back and through the misty whiteness Anthony looked like an Arctic explorer. His lips were cracked too, adding to the effect, and I called him 'Scott of the Antarctic' until I remembered what happened to Scott.

We headed upwards all the time, but it wasn't too steep now, just steady trudging towards the cairn marking the top of the pass. This was where the guidebook had promised spectacular views – 'A revelation of a new world … Standing on the borders of Italy and France, the views are magnificent …' – but all we could see was white sky, white land. We took photographs of each other at the cairn, standing in front of a bleak pile of stones.

It took longer than we thought it should to reach the refuge, at least another two hours, and then a wall of snow blocked the final ascent. We had to scramble up a steep crag on all fours, like mountain goats, to get around it. Afterwards I sat on my bunk bed and made a list of what I had been afraid of in the last few days: twisting an ankle, falling, being lost, being too exhausted to keep going, having a heart attack, failing, dying.

Anthony sat on the lower bunk with me, his back leaning against the wall. 'Do you want a bit of *Ulysses*?'

I said okay and I put my notebook down as he pulled his mobile phone out and found the place we were up to and started to read. The words flowed as they always did but I couldn't listen. Bloom was still coming back from the funeral – he was coming back from the funeral all day in *Ulysses* – and the rich words slipped off the sides of my glassy brain.

My stomach started to feel queasy. Something was wrong. I excused myself and jumped up and went to the smelly bathroom to wash my face with cold water, then, back in the room, slipped into my sheet bag and pulled up the doona. I felt unsettled in my skin. Nothing in me was in its right place. I started trembling. I tried to quell it but it only got stronger. I called out to Anthony on the top bunk.

He swung down and crawled onto the narrow mattress and wrapped his arms around me. I trembled more violently. The more I tried to stop, the worse it became.

'Do you want to keep going?'

'Yes. Absolutely. I'm just not doing another certain-death crossing, that's all.'


In the morning it was bitterly cold and the sky was spitting sleety snow. We had to keep going, no-one was allowed to stay at the hostel except in blizzard conditions. I put all my layers on, but my hands were painful and within minutes my fingers felt as if they were burning. I remembered our fingerless host on the first night. I stopped in the lee of an abandoned stone barn at the bottom of the crag and rifled through my backpack until I found a pair of thick, dirty socks. I pulled them on my hands and felt immediate relief. They would soon be wet, but it was better than nothing.

There was a steep snow slope, straight down with scree at the bottom – a minor-injury crossing. Anthony plunged down in front of me, long strides, heels dug in, and I followed, crunching and sinking through the powder.

At the bottom, there was a glacial valley and a wall of moraine; above, a glacier that had retreated from the valley after crushing trees and rocks in its path. Now it didn't look powerful; it was dirty and shrinking; it wouldn't be there at all in another few years – in fact, at the current rate of global warming, all Alpine glaciers will have disappeared by the end of the century. Cataracts tumbled down the cliffs, milky green-grey against the dark rock, a nineteenth-century painting come to life. The floor of the valley was covered in lateral moraine, with torrents and pools threading through blackish *tourbière*. There were disturbing plants with succulent dark-red stems and alien-looking flowers, resembling desert plants, without woody stems or leaves, as if the response to harshness – snow and ice, or dryness and heat – is the same.

There were two paths to choose from. Continue down the valley to Courmayeur, or turn up to the right along the high path. The guidebook advised, 'In the Himalaya, one would need to walk for many a long day to capture such a vision as you will see from this high path'. There was no question which path to take. I might never get to the Himalaya.

## Walking around the mountain

The path was narrow and steep and soon there were snow patches several hundred metres across, but I was resigned to them now. I strode across with care and some confidence. There were a few torrents to cross too, but I felt a rising sense of elation. I had done it yesterday – despite the after-trembles – and I was doing it today. The rain was gone, clouds swirled away leaving a brilliant sky. I slid the socks off my hands – all fingers intact. I bubbled with energy, my body was light. Anthony and I exchanged glances and smiled.

At an abandoned stone hut above a lake, we stopped for coffee. We were at 2303 metres, already higher than the highest mountain in Australia. I could see Mont Blanc, Aiguille du Combal, Glacier de Miage – I was up there with them. An eagle, two eagles, circled across the valley below me. The white peaks and ridges were cut-outs against the brilliant blue. Wreaths of clouds dangled lower down like lacy collars folded over layers of rock that had been heaved upwards and twisted and laid down again when the African and Eurasian tectonic plates collided.

I slung off my pack and leaned it against a rock and sat cross-legged on the grass. Anthony passed me the metal cup from the thermos and poured me a coffee. On the peaks in front of me there was fresh snow, fallen overnight, but now the sun was warm. I took off my hoodie and stuffed it in my backpack. I was as tall as the mountain, my soul was in the sky; I was as pleased with myself as I have ever been, higher than hawks and eagles, as high as Barney had flown over the hinterland of Queensland. Laying claim to the territory of eagles. Barney told me that once an eagle had swooped down and clung onto the top edge of his wing and screeched at him. It was huge, its talons 11 centimetres across – he knew this because it had pierced the fabric of his wing and he had measured the holes afterwards. It had flapped its giant wings, keeping up with him, letting go, grasping the fabric again, screeching its mighty warning at him again. Get out of my territory! Then I was afraid, Barney said.

We packed up, then walked to the top of the ridge, following the path above the abandoned hut. The Mont Blanc massif stretched in all its glory as far as we could see to the left. In the face of its soaring slopes and sheer cliffs and, to me, unclimbable white peaks, I was uncharacteristically silent. I knew this was what I had come for. To drink beauty, to devour it with every step.

After walking for half an hour, fierce with greedy success and still bursting with energy, I rounded a spur and came face to face with a solid wall of snow. It rose several metres straight up from the path. We were both shocked, not quite able to believe it was there for several seconds.

We retraced our steps and walked up the spur. The other side of it was a basin with a slope of nearly 80 degrees, covered in snow and ending in cliffs. Anthony stared at it, reckoned we could traverse the side of the basin, digging our boots sideways. I looked at the almost sheer slope.

'No way on earth,' I said.

We went back to the path and by then a group of young Czechs had arrived on the spur.

'There is a crossing,' one of the women said. 'It's down there, around the side of the snow wall. It's above a cliff, but it's short. It can be done.'

We scrambled down the path again and saw, down to the side, the snow-covered crossing about four metres in length. It was centimetres from the cliff edge. At first, I was relieved to see how short it was, but as I approached it I realised it was a 'certain-death'. My heart started thudding.

'I don't know if I can do it.'

'You can. Just take it easy. We're not turning back again.' Anthony's tone was different; for the first time he was putting pressure on me. I felt a bewildered sense of abandonment. He was always on my side. Now he wanted me to do something that terrified me and which could kill me.

I looked at it again. Perhaps. I should be able to do it. It was only four metres.

But it was on the edge of a cliff, an abyss that disappeared a hundred metres or more below. It was covered in icy snow, the path leading to it sloped steeply down and was slicked with icy mud. I couldn't even get a sure step on it.

Suddenly, Anthony stepped onto it, walked across and then was on the other side facing me. Confusingly, I have no memory of watching him cross, none at all, but I can remember him on the other side.

'You can do it,' he said. He looked impatient.

I edged down towards it. My arms and legs were watery, heart and stomach queasy. No part of me, except will, wanted to do this. One more step and I would be on the snowy, icy crossing above the cliff. I wobbled.

'I really can't do it.'

'Come on! It's just a few steps.'

I'm stepping, slipping, falling over the cliff.

I suddenly squatted on the path.

'I can't.' I felt stupid and ashamed.

Anthony sighed, looked pissed off. I sat there. I couldn't get up; my legs were too weak.

'Can you stand up.' It was more like an order than a question.

'No.'

I looked at him, pleading for him to see I couldn't do this. I saw something shift in him. Letting go.

'I'll have to come back over then.'

I had put him in danger by not being able to cross myself. He could slip and fall to his death this time. I watched him re-traverse the awful crossing, but again, I have no memory, except I know he teetered when he was back on my side because I was in his way in the middle of the narrow track.

'Move,' he said tersely, and I crawled away. It felt pathetic to crawl, no longer bipedal, but it was all I was capable of.

Then I stood, shaking, and went back up the path and around the spur where the Czechs were eating lunch.

'I couldn't do it,' I blurted out. 'I was too scared. We are going back to the other path.'

'That's okay. Safety always has to come first. You don't want to die for a walk,' said one of the young men. I was surprised at his serious and reassuring tone.

'You could wait and cross with us if you like,' he offered.

I smiled. 'Thanks, but I don't think it would help. If I slipped, I would grab one of you and you would go over as well.'

He grinned back at me and I was grateful. I looked at Anthony. He had changed his attitude, was no longer impatient.

We started walking back down the mountain straight away. It kept cycling through my mind; what if I had waited for a while, sat and breathed a while, could I have done it then? What if I faced it?

I talked all the way down, going over and over the moments. There were many more than I've written here, moments I've forgotten and moments I've left out because perhaps they don't matter. But then, all of it does matter, even what I've forgotten; it's just the way we make sense of things, selecting and discarding. Making a story.

The one moment that keeps coming back is the step that I didn't take. When I started talking to Barney about his story, I asked him what was the one moment that kept coming back to him. Of course I knew the answer; the moment he lost control of the wing. The moment when you have no power to do anything about what is happening to you. Obviously it cannot ever be told if it slips the other way, into eternal silence, but from this side of the moment, it sears into memory and can never be erased. Memory presents and relentlessly re-presents, a mad-making repetition, like a video on endless loop, a crazy internet meme. The mind is in charge of keeping us alive and tries its best to handle powerlessness over death. Over mortality. But it doesn't work, repetition doesn't normalise, it makes it worse. When I asked him if he dreamed about the accident, Barney said, yes, that moment, over and over, for nearly two years.

After two hours of descent, we reached the lower path that followed the river along the valley floor. We stopped at a grassy bank by the torrent and ate leftover baguette and cheese and drank the last of the coffee. It was a pretty picnic spot and I sat, leaning against a rock, glad to be alive.

That night, in Courmayeur, we lay on the bed in the hotel and talked about what to do: continue or call it quits. I still wanted to circle the Mountain. Perhaps the snow will melt, I argued. I didn't want to fail. Anthony pointed out patiently that more bad weather was forecast, more snow and, almost certainly, more 'certain-death' crossings. I suddenly capitulated. I had to let it go, the months of planning, the dream of success.

'I did find beauty though,' I said. 'And terror.'

'You were brave,' Anthony said.

'What do you mean?' I asked.

'Because you had the courage to tell the Czechs that you were afraid.'

I said it wasn't much for me to admit to being afraid; it was just the way it was. And for Anthony it wasn't much to cross above the abyss. I asked him if he'd been afraid and he said 'cautious, but not fearful'. His heart was not thumping and his limbs were as wiry and reliable as always. I can't avoid the truth. I didn't have the courage in the end for extreme beauty – and this is where it hurts. Anthony did, and my brother did. In fact, my brother does still. His story didn't end with his fierce attempts to walk again; there's more to tell.

# Lazarus

Jenny arrived back on the second day after the accident. She had snatched one-and-a-half anxious days with her father in Adelaide before flying halfway across the country to Brisbane and coming straight from the airport to the hospital. Barney saw the devastation on her face when she walked in and saw him, the companion and lover who had always been by her side, now hooked up to a frightening array of tubes and machines and looking like an old man in a paper gown, wrecked and beaten. Weirdly, he was wearing sunglasses so that he appeared to be pretending to be on holiday or a movie star trying to be incognito. She knew he was wearing the multifocal sunglasses because his ordinary reading glasses had been left in the car when he'd set out flying, but it still added a level of strangeness she could do without.

She told him she had rung their three children. Their eldest daughter – in New Zealand – would be coming over as soon as she could, but the other two – their son in Dubai and their other daughter in Budapest – probably wouldn't be able to make it for a while. That was all right. They would be there when they could.

They talked about practical arrangements. His car had been picked up from the launch site and brought home by his flying friends. One of them had met Jenny at the airport with it. And she had rung Kathy and asked her to tell the rest of us, so we all knew.

Barney told her about the rollator. Not the agony, none of the detail, just that he had moved to the door and back. He couldn't say 'walked'.

Jenny held his hand. 'Is there anything you need?'

'I'd like to get out of this paper outfit. Could you bring some T-shirts and shorts to wear. And my reading glasses from the car. And something nice to eat.'

She smiled. He had always appreciated her cooking.

He told her about the melting walls and the monkeys and she looked worried. He assured her it was okay; he knew they weren't really there; the nurses had explained they were hallucinations from the opioids.

'I don't know why people choose to take drugs,' he said. 'It's very unpleasant and confusing.' Jenny nodded. Neither of them had been part of the dope-smoking generation, even when they were young.

Other visitors came that day or the next day. Kevin, the Buddhist brother who lives nearby, came in – Barney didn't know if it was for the first time or again; and his friends who had been on the hillside with him arrived. He could see in their eyes that they really did feel for him. They all wanted to help, to run errands for Jenny, to bring food. He felt overwhelmed by their concern and kindness. To know that others felt his pain, or were at least affected and distressed by it, was a revelation. People love me, he thought with a surprised bewilderment, not just Jenny, but people. He had never known it before.

# Lazarus

On the fourth day after the accident – all time was measured from this new day zero – the physiotherapist and nurse brought him a pair of crutches. They were made of aluminium, light and shiny, but apart from that looked like crutches from an old war movie. He was one of the helpless wounded.

The nurse folded back his bedclothes and lifted Barney's legs over the side of the bed. He put one crutch under his right arm, keeping his arm around Barney while the physio placed the other crutch. They let him go and he was standing there, or rather balancing there, all his weight on the firm pads of the crutches, his legs dangling. His whole body was in pain as it hung there. As if he were on a crucifix.

Bloody crucifixes were everywhere in our childhood; the sagging, pain-wracked body hanging on a cross on walls, on rosary beads, around necks, on altars, in classrooms. Even in the kitchen. We laugh about it sometimes: that we ate our meals under the image of a bleeding, tortured body. It seemed normal, that nailed, dangling body, always pictured as still suffering, not dead yet.

Neither was he.

He had to do something. Focus on what the physio was saying.

'Swing the crutches forward. We will hold you up.'

He jerked the crutches forward about ten centimetres.

'Move your right foot.' The physio leaned down and touched his leg. 'Feel that. Move that leg.'

He couldn't feel the touch of her hand but he could see it, so he tried to direct his right foot to lift. He could not feel or direct anything below his knees but there was the faint muscle strength in his upper thigh. He managed a short slide of a few centimetres.

'Now the other foot.'

He slid his other foot, managing to lift it slightly. He was shuffling. He suddenly realised he looked like our father with Parkinson's disease, in the last few years of his life. How frustrated and helpless Dad must have felt; the impossible marshmallow fog between his brain and his feet, nerve messages blocked or sporadic; the overwhelming distress of being dependent.

He shuffled the other foot. Dolly steps. That was part of a game everyone used to play at Suntop primary school when he was a kid. Dolly steps, giant steps, polka steps, hops, jumps, skips – and then you had to freeze. 'Statues' it was called. It was all so easy then. In four shuffles he was upright, his crutches parallel under his arms.

'Swing the crutches again.' The implacable physio smiled at him. She slid the drip stand and the nurse carried the urine bag.

They kept going – swing, shuffle, shuffle, rest, swing – over and over, to the door. He was exhausted already. And even though he couldn't feel the floor or the physio's hand on his leg when she gave him a tap, his feet and legs were burning with pain. He knew it was referred pain from his spine, not his feet or legs, but that fact made no difference. It was constant, but the movement had made it worse. He wanted to lie down now.

The nurse and physio helped him turn and then he began the marathon back to his bed. When he finally reached it, he wanted to cry at how inviting it was, the thought of being able to lie down, of not having to make any more effort. The nurse and physio helped him back into bed and he pressed the opioid button. They left the ward, but came back after lunch and then again mid-afternoon, not the same nurse, but another with the same cheerful, determined air, forcing him on the marathon twice more that day.

## Lazarus

On the sixth morning, the sky out the windows was the same grey as the walls. Jenny wasn't due to arrive for a few hours. She couldn't come every day because she was still working and it was an hour-and-a-half drive from Murwillumbah to the hospital. The day would stretch interminably until she arrived.

The crutches had been left by his bed. He looked at them for a while and thought, I could just give up or I could give it a shot. The opioid tube was detached, although the cannula was still in his arm. Other than that, there was only the catheter and urine bag to manage. He pushed back his sheet and blanket, swung his legs over the side of the bed and reached for the crutches. He placed them under his arms, held the urine bag handle and gripped the crutch and handle together, steadied himself, stood upright. He took a deep breath, focused on the door of the ward – just four metres, he could do that – and swung the crutches forward in a jerky sudden jump like a nervous frog. Whew! He hadn't fallen.

He shuffled his feet forward. He teetered a little to the right and with a sudden snap of fear realised he couldn't make his feet or legs adjust. He leaned back on his crutch to the left and regained balance. He could only rely on his arms, nothing else.

He made it to the door and back again. He did it again just before lunch and twice more in the afternoon, feeling proud of himself. He began to let himself dream that it may be possible. He might walk.

The next day he was in more pain and more weary than ever. He tried to walk with the crutches again by himself but it was impossibly exhausting. Was this it? A painful shuffle on crutches across a room? Being almost completely dependent on others? He would rather be dead.

A nurse came in to give him his drugs. She asked him his full name before she gave him the Oxycontin and scribbled something on her chart.

'How are we today?'

'Not so good. Going backwards.'

'Don't overdo it. It's not about being tough and pushing through it. Keep trying, but take it easy.'

It was the beginning of realising that if he pushed himself, he paid for it next day with severe pain and exhaustion. Sometimes the most useful thing he could do was not to do anything at all.

On the ninth day, he woke up again in the grey room. The sun was shining outside. He was now sharing his room with an old man who complained about the breakfast and then about the nurses. He had been complaining since he arrived a few days before, and had been rude to the nurses several times. Barney felt both angry and ready to cry. How dare that bloke complain when everyone was looking after him. He should feel grateful. He looked at his own crutches and thought clearly, 'I am going to be able to walk. Without crutches. Without any help. I'm going to start right now.'

When he first told me this, I thought it was a reaction against the old man's whingeing, but he told me much later that he'd decided that he would stay alive and walk because people loved him. I have to admit that when he said that, 'because people loved me', it disconcerted me all over again. I still wasn't used to Barney using such words; it was going to be slow letting go of my old picture of him.

He sat up in bed and, using his thigh muscles, swung his legs over the edge. He sat there for a minute, breathing through the pain that always came more strongly when he moved. He clutched his urine pack and catheter in one hand. Then he pushed his bed trolley-table just out of reach towards the wall. He took a deep breath, and with his hands on the mattress, pushed himself upwards, his arm muscles trembling. It took huge effort – and fear – and then he was standing. His right leg was more painful than the left, and felt weaker. He was out of balance. He stood for a moment, adjusting his balance with his upper body, then with a lurching, sliding step, grabbed for the trolley table.

He held onto the table, regained his balance, breathed, then let go and lurched another step to the wall. Two steps without crutches!

Leaning on the wall on his right side, holding his urine bag in the other, he took another step, then another. He slid, lurched, all the way to the door. It felt as if he were wading against an almighty current that got ever stronger as he stepped. He turned himself around, using the wall to balance, and headed back to his bed. Each step became more and more difficult as he pushed against the heavy current. When he finally made it back to the bed, he felt as if he had climbed Mt Everest. He lay down, exhausted, but with a feeling of jubilation. Some steely determination had formed in him, along with an image of himself as an upright, walking man. He would use that image to teach his nerves, muscles, limbs, to walk again.

The physiology of walking is straightforward enough. According to the science, when you walk you become an inverted pendulum, your centre of mass, somewhere in the belly, describing the arc. As you plant your foot on the ground in front of you, the ground exerts a force back up your leg that slows you down and continues to slow you as you rise on that foot to the top of the arc. At this point, your active or kinetic energy is at a minimum, as it is in a pendulum, but your potential energy is at a maximum. There is a small millisecond stop at the top, the 'alleviation phase', then, as that knee buckles and releases stored elastic energy in the ankle tendons, the 'launching phase', you fall forward as the next step is taken with the other foot, using a passive rotation of the hip. The potential energy is changed to kinetic and accelerates you forward. That's all there is to it.

It's the same for everyone – although apparently Kenyan women have eliminated the tiny millisecond pause, which means they walk much more efficiently than anyone else. Despite the rest of us using the same biomechanics, each of us has a different gait – and different gaits for different moods. Because Barney could not direct his ankles or lower legs – that is, part of the biomechanical sequence was missing – he could really only take steps from his hips, so his gait was stiff, robot-like. Even to do that, he had to re-imagine how to walk. He watched people walking, studied their movement, so he could imagine the correct shape of walking. If he had the picture in his mind, he reasoned, eventually his body must learn to follow.

The day after his first wall walk, Barney managed the two metres from bed to wall without the trolley-table. The next day, the three metres from the end of the wall to the bathroom door. Apart from traversing these chasms, he stayed near the walls, and then in another few days, he made it to the corridor where there were railings. The vinyl floor gleamed ahead of him like a pathway towards the nurses' station. He held the railings with one hand and shuffled up the corridor towards it. It was as slow as wading through mud, which became thicker as he walked. Several nurses and other patients stopped to watch him, admiring his progress. Near the station he thought he really couldn't move his legs against the thick blur. But he did, stepping and sliding, he made it all the way to the station and back. He had walked 40 metres!

'I'm walking,' he told Jenny that afternoon. She was thrilled for him but not all that surprised. She knew what he was like.

Over the next three weeks, he walked along the walls of the hospital, took the lift downstairs and walked in the foyer, and then one day, after three weeks, tried the stairs. Although he was slowly walking further, the rate of improvement slowed every day, and some days he regressed and could only walk half as far as he had the day before. He had to stay near the wall and had to be careful not to catch or tangle his catheter tube when he passed a door handle or another patient, as he got a painful reminder that the tube was attached to his bladder.

The muscles on his thighs were starting to strengthen, but below the knees he was 'free-wheeling', the bottom half following the motion of his hips. There was still no use of the muscles in his calf, ankles or feet, which, he realised, were the muscles that had adjusted minutely all the time to keep him upright. He walked without holding the walls, but near enough to fall on them if he lost balance. There was no way to correct even the slightest teeter. Some days he still overdid it and suffered the next day with severe pain and exhaustion. It was difficult not to try too hard.

But he would try again the following day. Every day, four times a day, up and down the corridors, around the foyer. He became a familiar sight in the spinal unit; his thin, determined body, in T-shirt and shorts now hanging a bit loose, pacing by. One of the unit's success stories. The medical staff knew that only half of patients with spinal cord injuries ever walked again.

Four weeks after he fell out of the sky, he decided to walk from the hospital a couple of blocks to the barber to get a haircut. He always liked to look tidy and neat, and anyway, it would be good practice. It was probably against the rules to leave the hospital grounds, but the doctor had told him he would be allowed home in a few days, so he would need to be able to get out and walk down the street if he wasn't to be housebound for the rest of his life. He dressed in his usual T-shirt, shorts and gym shoes – the compression bandages were gone – and took the lift down to the foyer. There was no point in tiring himself out with stairs before he even started.

He stepped out the glass front doors of the hospital and stopped for a moment – it felt good to feel the late spring sun and the soft moist air of Brisbane on his skin – then looked up to see the whole arc of the sky above him. It was the first time since the accident that he had seen the vastness of the sky that had been his home, the place where he felt most himself. He could see a bird high up, dark coloured, perhaps a crow. A sky creature.

But he had to keep his gaze at ground level. The lawns around the hospital stretched down to the main road and the footpath was slightly sloping so he walked even more slowly than usual, and there was nothing to grab onto if he lost his balance. When he came to a driveway sloping across the direction of his walking, he stopped. He realised he couldn't cross it without falling over. He could not make his ankles adjust for the slope. He stepped with care off the footpath and walked on the road around the driveway then stepped back up onto the footpath. This was going to be his way of crossing driveways for well over a year; sensation and use of any muscles in his lower legs did not start returning for 15 months.

But he wasn't there yet. Not even at the barber. He had to cross busy Ipswich Road to the shopping centre. He waited for the lights to change then started to cross. He walked as fast as he could in his shuffling stiff-legged style, but even going 'flat-out', as he put it, the lights changed back while he was still halfway across. To his surprise, the cars waited for him to reach the safety of the other side without revving or honking. Perhaps they had seen his red hospital wristband, or recognised in his gait that he was doing the best he could. It took him over 45 minutes to cover the 300 metres from the hospital, a distance that would take me less than five minutes.

He reached the barber with its red, white and blue pole painted on the front window and pushed into the shop, relieved to be able to sit down. When it was his turn, he confessed to the barber that he had gone AWOL from the hospital. 'Yes, I know,' she said drily, looking at his wristband. When he finally made it back to the hospital, this time crossing the highway on the overpass, which he hadn't noticed before but which required climbing stairs, he was exhausted and in severe pain. Still, when one of the nurses complimented him on his haircut, he couldn't help boasting he had walked down the street to the shopping centre to get it.

Just over four weeks after the accident, Barney was released from hospital and Jenny arrived to drive him home to Murwillumbah. He got out of the car in his driveway by himself and walked slowly up the steps into his own house.

Everything in the house was glowing – Jenny always kept everything neat and fresh. It was the way he liked it and, in fact, he often did it himself, making sure everything was orderly. Sun streamed in onto wooden floors, his paintings were bright and cheerful on the walls. Even though he was still in almost constant pain – and would be for more years than he could have borne to imagine – and he still had the catheter and urine bag to manage – at least he was home. He had only been away a month and everything around him was the same, but it was a lifetime since he had been here; his old life had been taken away from him and he still had to work out how to make a new one. The Fates had smacked him out of the sky, dropped the thread holding him up, but he was up and ready to shake his fist and give it another shot.

# The Fates

The Fates have a lot of bad press, they're always doing something low or tragic, but I like them. I'm not trying to stay on their good side – I would if I could – but I am impressed with the idea of them. They're deeper than an idea; more a dark pool under conscious thought, born of the knowledge of having come from non-existence for no known reason, and the dread of having to return to it. We're in the daylight for such a short time, in sun and rain and wind, with a bloody raw heart, drowning in babies' unprotected eyes, lost in lips and skin, power sparkling from our hands as we build blinding cities; how can all this disappear? Then lightning strikes, avalanches fall, wars explode, cars crash, illness shrivels, addiction splits, and all that is precious is taken away.

There must be someone we can persuade to let our dear ones stay longer, someone we can propitiate, someone who knows when the thunder will roar. The Fates, the Moirai, holding the threads of our destiny, they know: Clotho who spins the threads, Lachesis who blindly hands them out – a black, knotty one for you, a shiny golden one for you – and Atropos who cuts all the threads in the end. But the Fates are implacable, they cannot be persuaded. No-one can escape the Fates, not even the Gods.

I like the toughness of this idea. No, not *like*, that's the wrong word; it's terrifying, but on a good day I admire its truthfulness. Things happen and no amount of pleading or offerings will make any difference. It takes such courage to live without a story that will save you. Barney wouldn't talk about it in terms of the Fates or Destiny – it would be making too much of it – but I can't help seeing things that way; the story that explains what happened, images that make the heart quiver, the traces of our journeys. It's where Barney's story and mine weave together, not in time or place, but in the tangle of threads, which we imagine we have created. I'm nowhere near tough enough to willingly accept whatever threads the Fates spin and hand out – let alone cut – but I understand the need and the pleasure of making threads and of placing them in a pattern.

When I look at the paths Barney has traced in the sky – and I can see them clearly on his computer track-log – and mine scribbled in my scruffy notebooks, I can see now how much they echo each other. We both have endless practical matters to take care of before we start – careful packing of equipment, weather reports, fitness, we both climb upwards with effort, circling around the mountain, we both teeter on the edges of cliffs made of air or rock, and on occasion we both soar with the unbelieving eagles in weightless joy.

And then there's our recording of our journeys. It's not enough for either of us to traverse the earth or the sky and know their wonders; we both must keep note of it. Although his records are computerised and mine are handwritten in small notebooks, we both record dates, distances, location, altitude profiles. It's a compulsion that we share, a need to keep evidence – although neither of us knows why. Scratching 'I was here' on the slippery surface of existence?

And there is the natural world we both long to dissolve into. For Barney it's eagles and hawks, the intricate sky, the spread-out geography of earth, endlessly patterned; for me it's magpies and sparrows, eucalypts and oaks, rocks, a close-up view in the folds of the intricate earth. It strikes me that Barney's view is more god-like than mine. He sees the wide view, the vast unity of earth and sky; I see the ground beneath my feet.

I notice the colour of rocks: grey, purple, white, black, pink: I notice the shapes: some are geometrically regular and pleasing – I like ovals best – some resemble other things. I have one which is an almost exact map of Australia; most are random, uneven shapes. I notice textures – silky smooth, granular, glassy – and I spend a foolish amount of time as I walk trying to recall names from high school geology – basalt, granite, quartz, limestone, sandstone – and trying to decide what formed them: volcanic activity, glaciers, metamorphic pressure. Sometimes I take photographs of them, thinking that later I will identify them. Often I bring one or two home with me, zipped into the side pocket of my pack.

But there are other rocks, huge boulders sitting on the surface and monoliths rooted in the earth, which I have visited as well. Baron Rock, the monolith behind my childhood farm for a start. And the Remarkable Rocks on Kangaroo Island off the coast of South Australia, the hooked eagle rock leaning towards the sea, the wind-worn bones of mythical creatures curving over the rock platform, the lacy boulders a dreamscape of orange lichen and sandstone.

And then there is Uluru, the vast rock temple in the middle of the Australian continent. For a long time I wanted to walk around the Rock; I wanted to see it and touch it and circumnavigate it. When I finally did see it, from above first as I flew in over it, it looked like a bare red heart in the desert, something exposed and necessary. The ground level view, the Uluru shape, had been there from earliest childhood, ochre against blue, a rough oblong rising out of the flat desert. That moment, looking down at it, it was unrecognisable.

# The Uluru offering

The way that memory comes into the present is not in a dated time sequence. Memory isn't logical, it's not ordered by time or place; events don't present themselves in months and years with an unending forward movement. But neither are they random, although they often seem to be when they first present. Memory is deeply structured in its images, symbols, smells, colours, sounds, tastes; all circling, repeating, spiralling, like poetry. Like Barney's track-log. With each circle on his log, it's hard to tell whether he is in the same location in relation to the paddocks below, just higher up, or whether he is, in fact, further along. It's not until I zoom in close on the computer that I can see it unfurl and stretch out in space and time. In his unfurled story, time is measured in minutes of pain and hours of learning to walk a little further every day; the dates do not line up neatly with my walking. But if there needs to a be date, then the day I walked around Uluru was four years after Barney's fall.

# The JOY of HIGH PLACES

Uluru had always seemed impenetrable, unknowable. Its shape was too familiar, like the shape of your own child's face. It was a picture I had seen too many times. Whenever an image comes first, the original gradually becomes impossible to see or know with any intimacy. But I wanted to try.

I had a Rock in my childhood, so I did know something about the nature of rocks. Baron Rock wasn't on our farm, it was on Harry Wykes' place, but it's at the centre of my family's mythology of place. The lopsided egg shape of it – I know I can speak for Barney and all of us – is the oldest and deepest shape in our lives. And a repeated image in my writing. My sense of being is unimaginable without it hunched there underneath all my memories like the bottom-most turtle holding up the world.

When I walked towards it with my brothers and sisters, scrambling over the wire fence into Harry's farm, we always called out to it. We had to wait until we were halfway across Harry's paddock to get a response, although we often impatiently called before then.

'Hallooo,' we yelled.

'Allooo,' it called back in its clear cool stone voice, not quite catching the first consonant of the greeting. Ah, I cannot tell you how wonderful it is to have a Rock speak back to you. Such a clear cool voice our Rock had.

Jung wrote, 'no voices now speak to man from stones, plants and animals, nor does he speak to them thinking they can hear', but we called out and our stone answered. Our hearts stretched, our skinny chests expanded, and we started to run; always we ran when the Rock answered.

Baron Rock, I understood later in geography class, was made of solidified lava, the weathered basalt heart of a volcano left after millions of years had worn down the crater and revealed the volcanic plug. Rain running over its sides had created a small micro-environment around its base – native pines, eucalypts, native grasses – and on the rock itself, pale green-grey and orange lichens and small ti-trees grew in crevices.

The front was too steep to climb so we walked through the pines and gums until we came to a cleft in the rocks we could scramble up. We were on our own with no-one to worry that we were too near the edge, so we skittered like large lizards across the rocks, trying to find the quickest way up. We stood with the wind in our hair, with hawks, and sometimes eagles, circling nearby. It was the first time the joy of high places coursed through me.

But that didn't mean I wanted to climb Uluru all these years later. For the local Anangu people, Uluru is a sacred site, which they ask visitors not to climb. But even given my love of high geography, I didn't have any desire to climb it. Climbing to the top seemed an act of domination. I wanted the opposite, to submit myself to the Rock Heart, to walk around it, head bowed, to feel the passing of the Rock at a walking pace, step by step on the earth.

In Tibetan Buddhism there's a practice called *kora*, circling the mountain. You walk clockwise around the mountain paying homage to its sacred being. The more powerful the site, the more merit can be gained. Prostration, lying flat on the ground after each step, produces greater rewards than simply walking – apparently the practice can expunge the sins of a lifetime – but I was hoping walking might be enough for someone who was not so much a sinner as a non-believer.

Belief looks real, so elaborated with stories and rituals and sacred objects – I love all that – but it depends on accepting the stories of ethereal beings and gods and ancestors walking the earth without verifiable evidence. That sounds so dry – *verifiable evidence* – so snooty and superior even, but after a childhood of faith in God, and then decades of faith in an amorphous Higher Reality, now it seems everything could be explained as brilliant constructions of our brilliant minds. I like the stories still, the rituals, but they are artefacts, like stone carvings and painted mandalas in a museum. Now I can be happy with a few facts.

The geological facts of Uluru, and Kata Tjuta, the domed rocks nearby, are a fantastical story. Both rock formations lie on the southern edge of the Amadeus Basin, a depression on the earth's surface, which, twice over hundreds of millions of years, has been a shallow sea. The elusive Inland Sea the explorers searched for in the early days of British colonisation really did exist; they were just 300 million years too late for it.

After the sea receded the first time, the buckling earth created the Petermann Ranges, bare mountains that eroded into two vast fans, one rocky, the other sandy. A second shallow sea covered the fans in mud and sand and, over time, the pressure turned the fans to stone. About 300 million years ago, the sea receded and the earth buckled again in its restless way, twisting the two fans on their sides. The rocky fan became the conglomerate Kata Tjuta, and the sandy fan, the arkose sandstone of Uluru; both of them red due to iron in the rock oxidising as it came in contact with the air. So there we have it, Uluru is the edge of an ancient red fan that once lay under a primeval sea. Anything is possible.

The red fan is over 2000 kilometres from where I live in Sydney and it took more than three hours to fly there. Somewhere below me, Baron Rock dreamed on, quiet now I suppose, without any children to talk to. From above, the geometry of paddocks shifted to the organic curves of a landscape where humans were barely noticeable. The amoeba-like shapes of vegetation and claypans, red and grey-green and cream, floated on the surface. By the time Anthony and I arrived at Uluru, it felt as if we were in another country.

In this new country there was thigh-high spinifex, creamy-white, covering the red earth as far as the eye could see, purifying all the elements of the landscape. Red sand, pale jade sage bush, narrow desert oaks, mulga, cassia, occasional white-skinned gums, all bound together by a wash of soft spinifex – and above, an infinite sky.

It looks like a simple ecosystem, reduced to fundamentals, but there are more than 400 species of native plants in the region of Uluru. The local Anangu divide the fauna into *Puni* (trees), *Puti* (shrubs), *Tjulpuntjulpunpa* (flowers) and *Ukiri* (grasses). One of the most distinctive trees is the *Kurkara*, or desert oak, which is Christmas tree–shaped when it's young, and the shape of a small English oak when it's mature. Their dark green leaves looked fresh against the silvery grey of the *Wanari* mulga. I saw Sturt's Desert Pea, red and black and pointed like pixie hats, in the gardens around the unit where we were staying, but didn't see any that weren't cultivated.

The flora here has to be able to survive on just 300 mm of rain each year. That's half the annual rainfall of central western NSW where I grew up, which was just enough, some years, to grow wheat and oats and lucerne. Here, no European crops would be likely to germinate, let alone survive. The average temperature for six months of the year is over 30 degrees Celsius, so what moisture there is doesn't last long in the desiccating heat. At night in winter, as Europeans call the season, the air temperature is cold enough for frost and dew to settle on leaves and grasses, and once, in July 1997, slushy snow fell on Uluru. I've only seen photographs of it; the snow and grey clouds and waterfalls pouring off the Rock made it look like a vast and wild fortress fit for a European story.

The Anangu seasons are differentiated not by rainfall or temperature nor climatic conditions of any kind, but by what foods are available. The Anangu say there are five seasons: *Itjanu* is from January to March; *Wanitjunkupai* is April and May; *Wari* is late May, June and July; *Piriyakutu* is August and September, then *Mai Wiyaringkupai* around December. According to the seasonal timetable, the Anangu look for bush tomatoes, wild figs, wild oranges, conkerberries, mulga apple, wild passionfruit, in a landscape where I can see no food.

It was *Wanitjunkupai* when we arrived there, warm and sunny with a cloudless blue sky. At sunset we watched the looming Rock change from ochre to deep glowing red, and the sky from cerulean to duck-egg blue and pink. Cameras on tripods and phones clicked dozens of times. Every snap yielded a postcard perfect version of the monolith, its simplicity of form impossible to get wrong.

'Is it just a Big Rock?' I said. It was my secret fear. Not a temple, not a sacred mountain, not the beating heart keeping the land alive.

'Yeah, it's a Big Rock,' said Anthony. He made it sound as if that was all it needed to be. 'Bigger than the pyramids anyway, by far. The Great Pyramid is less than 150 metres high, and Uluru is nearly 350 metres.'

'Well, I just want to walk around it,' I said.

# The Uluru offering

That night at the pub we read *Ulysses* – it was still travelling with us – and Anthony read quietly in the fake Irish accent he had developed:

Why did Bloom experience a sentiment of remorse?

Because in immature impatience he had treated with disrespect certain beliefs and practices.

As?

The prohibition of the use of fleshmeat and milk at one meal, the hebdomadary symposium of incoordinately abstract, perfervidly concrete mercantile coexreligionist excompatriots: the circumcision of male infants; the supernatural character of Judaic scripture; the ineffability of the tetragrammaton; the sanctity of the Sabbath.

How did these beliefs and practices now appear to him?

Not more rational than they had then appeared, not less rational than others' beliefs and practices now appeared.

'I'm tired,' I said.

We set our alarm and got up in the dark next morning. I put on my walking gear and hefty boots, the ones that turn the planet under my heels, then we drove to Mala car park on the dark side of Uluru. The Rock loomed even larger than it had the day before, taking up most of the sky in front of us. It was before dawn, cool and fresh, but there was already a pale light as we shrugged on our daypacks, checked our water bottles and headed off along the track.

At the beginning was a gate in front of metal posts, and chain that led up the Rock for those who wanted to climb. A sign said the Anangu people asked visitors not to climb, and next to it there was another sign indicating the climb was closed today because it was too windy at the top. But there was a woman climbing, about 20 metres up. A ranger appeared from nowhere and yelled, 'Come down from there'. I slipped my hand into the pocket of my pants, feeling the small stone I had brought with me from my cup of stones at home.

I've collected stones for years. Not often, just when I spot one that speaks to me. The first ones I picked up came from a beach on the coast south of Sydney decades ago when I was young with Anthony, and they seemed immediately to be talismans that would protect us and our lives together. It was just a feeling, not a thought-out cosmology; at that time I knew nothing about the idea of stones as powerful or sacred. The stone that represents me is like a flattened egg or lingam, an oval shape with swirling stripes of black and brown metamorphosed sandstone; Anthony's stone, I'm a bit embarrassed to say because it's overly obvious, looks like a slightly flattened penis. On another visit to the same beach, I found two more stones, one for each of our sons; both of them elongated ovals of slate with threads of quartz through them, like veins in skin. I keep them all in an old painted cup on a windowsill in my study and occasionally take them out and hold them in the warmth of my palm, a private ritual of protection.

I like the European walking tradition of placing stones in piles along the wayside. Stone piles probably started as a practical method of clearing stones off the path, but it's become a ritual, honouring the landscape. They are often a kind of altar, acknowledging that this is a holy place. There are piles on high mountain passes, in front of grottoes, where someone has died, where a story has happened. Sometimes walkers bring stones from home and carry them all the way along the path and leave them at the end. At times stones are carried as a symbol of someone – as Jung said, soul-stones – or they are carried and left in a particular location to symbolise an inner letting go.

Jung wrote that ancient peoples in many cultures collected certain stones as symbols of the life force, with the power to protect and create. The stones linked those who held them with ancestors and with place, and could even bring new life. The 'Australian aborigines', he said, rubbed a 'child-stone' with a tjuringa, a carved stone of sacred power, to make a new baby leap into the womb. He confessed that as a child he had 'long kept a stone in my trouser pocket' which he then hid in his attic with a manikin he made, and he visited and held it whenever he felt disturbed. It made him feel safe and calm, no longer at odds with himself.

I have long kept all my stones, but a couple of days before leaving for Uluru I realised that I wanted to bring an offering with me. It didn't take long before I knew it had to be one of the stones. Not my family stones, not even in the coldest light of rationality would I part with them, but I had other stones spilling around the cup, which I had picked up when I was walking in Australia and in Ireland, France, England, Italy. They were my connection to Australia where I was born on country, and to Europe where my long-ago ancestors had been born. On my second Camino walk in Spain I had carried one of them from

Australia and left it on a vast pile of stones placed by pilgrims from all over the world at the Cruz de Ferro. It was a custom that had been practised for centuries. I didn't know what it originally meant and I hadn't felt any particular connection to the geographic place, but I did think about the people who had passed by there for a thousand years. All their stones nestled together there, connecting them across time and countries of origin.

I looked at my stones, and held them and remembered where I had found them. The one I selected as an offering was a flat oval stone, a pale grey schist, about three centimetres by two, a good shape for skimming over water and small enough to slip into a pocket.

The stone came from a creek in the Snowy Mountains, a low range that had once been a sea-bed dotted with volcanic islands. Much more recently ice ages had created glaciers, which carved out valleys and lakes and left glacial moraine in dramatic piles. It had been made of sea and fire and ice, and then eons had worn it down into a vast plateau dissected by deep gorges. I had walked in the Snowies at Easter three years earlier and had bent down to pick up this stone from the cold water, drawn by its smoothness and its small quiet shape.

It lay in my pocket as I began walking, heading northwards and clockwise around the Rock, a crisp wind blowing back my hair. The path was close to the rock wall, which was red even in the pre-dawn light and filling one side of the sky. I touched the rock, just the once, palm against stone. Even though the air was cold, the rock was warm. The path snaked ahead, inviting circumnavigation, but apart from Anthony, there was no one else in sight.

I snapped a picture of the white spinifex rippling in the

wind in contrast with the red rock and the stunted green gums, and was surprised to see a skull shape in the stone. Afterwards I kept seeing shapes in the stone: a large fish, an elephant's head, a Cappadocian cave-house, a screaming Edvard Munch face, ghost men in a cave, a brain, a heart, sexual organs – especially female. But I stopped taking pictures because the places I was most inclined to see shapes and faces were also the places the Anangu had designated as sacred. I couldn't help thinking that we all want the earth to speak to us. To tell us something, anything.

We came to Kantju Gorge, a narrow valley in the flank of Uluru. As I walked in, the wind dropped suddenly. The sides of the valley undulated like upright sand dunes, creating a feeling of enclosure in solid waves. Deep in the 'V' of the gorge there was a waterhole with a sign saying that it was a place to be quiet and to listen. I stood and stared at the dark water for a while and felt the flat stone in my pocket. Anthony, who had been walking several metres ahead of me, came back and stood beside me.

'This place has a very strong feeling of stillness and silence,' he said.

'That's what it says on the sign,' I said.

'Okay, well I didn't read that.'

'Probably just that the wind is stilled in here,' I said.

After the gorge, the path swung out away from the base of the Rock to avoid sites that were sacred to Anangu men. We were on the sunny north-eastern side now but it was still cool. A series of scooped-out dry pools cascaded down from the top, ending in a drop to the desert floor that must have been spectacular in the rain. All the caves and crevices had been created by millions of years of wind and rain; the course of water marked a greenish black by the algae that grew when it did rain. How determined is life to take advantage of such rare water!

The path had widened and was patterned with other boot prints and bike tracks. The orangey-red dust scuffed under my boots, coated them, made them part of the landscape. I looked down and saw a line of caterpillars, head-to-toe, making a kind of caterpillar train over a metre long and as straight as a ruler. I looked them up later; they are called 'processionary caterpillars' and they follow a silken thread the lead caterpillar exudes. The spikily furry creatures looked so purposeful, plodding seemingly from nowhere to nowhere.

On the sunrise side of the rock, it was warmer, with no shade. The air was dry and clear, parching to the throat and mouth. It was about four kilometres to the eastern end, the bottom of the heart, a straight stretch with nowhere to fill water bottles – we had stocked up with extra bottles so there was no chance of running out – but it did make me think about the white explorers trying to traverse this country with no knowledge of how to survive. And how did the Anangu survive with rare rainfall and only two shrinking water holes? Of course, they knew and still know the country so intimately that they could find moisture in hollows and soakages and even tree roots and, in winter, dew on the leaves of the sage bush and grasses. To me it was a country I could lay myself down on with awe, prostrate myself in wonder, but anything less than that – simple daily life – seemed impossible.

The path here was about 200 metres from the base, which was a better position for seeing the rock, although I still wanted to be closer to it. It was its presence I wanted more than the view. It was on this side that I saw the Munch face, twisted and anguished; and the brain, eroded high up on the wall of rock. I thought, I cannot hear the Anangu stories, but the stone is telling me stories in a language I can hear, using metaphors and similes I can interpret. If the Rock is a sacred text, perhaps it speaks in different languages to all who come.

We reached the eastern end, domed like a giant stupa – the red stone and blue sky more still and silent than I could have imagined. There was not even the promise of revelation that I had felt before in the bush. It felt older and more inaccessible than anything my twenty-first-century brain could know. I touched the oval stone in my pocket, but there was no answering pull.

We set off into the heat along the southern side, the sun high enough now to light the whole rock. A formation like a giant fish, with small eyes and an open cave-mouth, gulping air, dwarfed the gums in front of it. In another couple of kilometres we reached a sign, Kuniya Walk, indicating another rock gorge. We followed the path into what, in this geography, could be called a glade – it had green grasses, cassia, white-skinned eucalypts, a little bridge and, high above, a love-heart carved by nature in the rock. At the end of the glade, at the bottom of a set of dry pools cascading down the rock, was the Mutitjulu Waterhole. The water was dark, shaded by the rock overhead, which was also in shade until near the top where the light transformed it into a pink glow. The whole effect was feminine; the folds of flesh-coloured rock, the creases, the dampness, the fronds of grasses.

Ah, I thought, this is the place. I curled my hand around the stone in my pocket. It was warm in my palm, it fitted snugly. The sign near the waterhole told the story of the python woman

Minyma Kuniya who defeated the warrior Wati Liru and then her spirit combined with her nephew's to become Wanampi, the water snake. Wanampi controlled the water and would let it flow when the Anangu sang to her.

People came and went, looking at the water hole, looking up at the shaded rock and the sunlit rock-flesh above, staring for a while. I waited. I didn't want anyone to see me make my offering, not wanting anyone to think I was just throwing stones. I kept my hand on the stone, thinking about my stories, my family, how they had come to this country with a red heart in the middle of it. I was the first one of my family to come here to the centre; this was our offering, a small flat stone. It was from us, from everywhere we have put our roots into the soil. We are mixed in with this place now.

I threw the small stone and it plopped in the mud near the pool. Immediately afterwards, and with a sharp pang, I thought, I should have asked the Anangu if it was all right to bring a gift like that. I was too absorbed in my own story to have thought of it before. In my set of stories it was a humble offering; in the Anangu stories it could be an intrusion, even a violation. It's only a little stone, I told myself, made of the elements, made from the same earth, from the same history of sea and fire and ice, but the fact stuck like a pebble in a shoe; I didn't ask. I had enacted my story and didn't take account of theirs; it was the whole dark story of colonisers who never asked, compressed in one little stone. The stone is there now, sitting on the edge of a muddy waterhole at Uluru. I can feel it there in my heart, scraping uneasily.

# Phoenix

When Barney announced that he intended to fly again, I couldn't believe it. Surely he was announcing a fantasy, a longing that could only be fulfilled in an ideal world, not something he would actually do. Now that falling out of the sky and being smashed to pieces wasn't a mere theoretical possibility but knowledge lived in a body in daily pain, how could he take a step off the earth again?

It's easy to understand the pull of high places, the physical sense of liberation. One year I walked over a range of mountains in Spain, the Sierra de O Courel mountains in Galicia, which held none of the terror of Mont Blanc but were still rough and wild. Each step up the mountain stretched calf and thigh muscles. With each step my foot '*épousait la terre*', married the earth, as a Frenchman at the *refugio* where I stayed the night before told me it must, and each time my boot pulled the rotating planet towards me. I was eating the mountain.

The gravel path underfoot crunched and shifted beneath my thick boots. It wasn't hot but my body was sweating. Bare arms pulled downwards on the walking poles and palms were damp on the cork grips. I'd been walking for two hours, nearly all of it up the mountain.

I rounded a steep corner and the slope on the right side of the path fell steeply away so that my line of sight was high above the trees and for the first time the vastness of the Sierra de O Courel was revealed. There were mountains and valleys rolling away as far as the eye could see; endless folding of light and shade, threads of mist, sun on beech and oak forests and on small meadows. And above, a vast dome of blue.

I remembered a dream from decades ago; a walking dream, not flying. I was striding up a mountain path that fell away, crumbled, behind me. I could only keep going upwards. Ahead, beyond the mountain top, on the other side, angelic choirs were singing. When I reached the top, golden rays streamed out from the land beyond the mountain as the angelic chorus swelled. In the dream, my heart felt near to breaking.

In the struggle upwards, in real life, that is, I began to feel the same sense of glory. Joy shafted through my body like light spilling into an old dusty room. Anthony, who was walking ahead, stopped at a rocky platform overhanging the mountainside. He gazed across the ranges rising and falling all the way to the horizon. I stopped beside him.

'All I need now is an angelic choir,' I said. He had forgotten the dream, if I ever told him, and shrugged.

'This must be the version of the world your brother gets when he flies,' he said.

'Birds see it every day,' I said.

We took photographs of each other on our phones; light exploding around us, arms wide, archangels with walking poles, lords of all we surveyed.

We stepped back on the path, and around the next outcrop of rocks the village of O Cebreiro was nestled into the top of the mountain. It had cafes and an auberge, a souvenir shop and a chapel. And cars. It's not hard to drive to the top of the mountain.

Anthony walked off in search of coffee and I went into the chapel. In the 1300s, when an unbelieving priest was saying mass here, the bread and wine changed into actual flesh and blood and the blood flowed out of the chalice. It wasn't any old chalice, it was the Holy Grail, the cup that Jesus drank from at the Last Supper, hidden here in the Middle Ages. The Holy Grail is gone now – no surprise there – but there was a crystal reliquary with alleged remains of flesh and blood, although I couldn't see any identifiably bloodthirsty bits. The chapel was empty of worshippers despite the macabre miracle, but there was a CD playing, a choir singing the Hallelujah Chorus. I stood for a while, then went out to find Anthony.

'There's a choir of angels in the chapel,' I said.

I kept remembering that Barney had wished he'd been killed outright in the fall. It's a confronting thing to hear a brother – anyone – say. No-one wants to think death is not the worst thing. Barney had repeated a number of times he would have chosen death over being 'crippled', his word, and being in constant severe pain. But now he was walking slowly, albeit in severe pain, he no longer had to use a catheter, his bowels were more-or-less working, he was alive. How could he even imagine risking it all again?

He had seen a woman wheelchair flying several times over the years. She arrived at the launch site in a van with a team of at least two people, usually three, and a long, low wheelchair with three wheels. One person helped attach the harness and arranged the wing and the others waited by the chair to either hold it back or give it a push, depending on what was needed. Like everyone else, Barney had admired her courage and determination, but even before he had begun learning how to walk again, he knew he didn't want to fly unless he could do it by himself. He wanted to be able to manage all the stages: setting up, taking off, landing on his feet and carrying his gear afterwards, without having to rely on others – it was that or nothing.

His flying friends – Gavin, Drew, and others – came to visit him regularly, and phoned and emailed, mostly enquiring about his progress, but also to talk about flying. They didn't steer away from the topic and Barney didn't want them to. He was having recurring nightmares about the crash – always the moment he lost control and the helpless moments that followed – and he would continue to have them for two years, but he wanted to hear about flying. He couldn't do it, couldn't even run, and still didn't think he ever would, but he wanted to hear the stories about being aloft, up there in the sky. It was his world.

In the first week after he arrived home from hospital, he measured out a 100-metre course along his veranda, down the steps and around his backyard, and began training several times a day. By the end of that week he could walk 300 metres without stopping. It took half an hour and his gait was an oddly straight-legged shuffle, but he could do it. It must have looked strange, the thin man stepping out with unnatural determination, around and around his garden every morning and every afternoon. 'I suppose I looked like a robot,' he said. 'My stiff-legged walk.'

# Phoenix

I never saw him at his practise, but, when I imagine it, I see it from above; a small figure circling an enclosure in a small town in the hinterland of northern New South Wales, a not-yet striding figure wrenching back his destiny from the Fates.

Three months after the fall, he could walk a whole kilometre without stopping, although it still looked more like a shuffle. He had been concentrating on increasing how far he could walk, and how fast, but now he started to think about gait, and about running. He still could not feel his feet, not even the sensation of the ground underfoot, and wouldn't for another year, which meant he could not direct his feet. Nor could he direct his lower leg muscles, his calf and ankle muscles. He watched people walk, trying to analyse how a natural gait was achieved. It wasn't that he wanted to avoid looking odd, but he knew that if he looked as if he were walking naturally it probably meant he was exercising the right muscles and training the right nerves. Because he didn't have the muscle control to do what everyone else was doing without thinking about it, he came up with a way to achieve it.

Before the accident, Barney and Jenny had both been keen ballroom dancers. It was Jenny's passion, but Barney had gone along to please her and applied his usual methodical attention until he was a skilled dancer. He could waltz, foxtrot, salsa, rumba and swing with the best of them. In fact, he and Jenny had done dance 'exams' and won ostentatious trophies in both ballroom and Latin dancing. Once when I visited them, Barney had opened their wardrobe and shown me his outfits of shiny shirts, vests, narrow black pants and pointy-toed shoes alongside Jenny's multi-coloured dresses of froth and glitter. They had gone out dancing two or three times a week.

# The JOY of HIGH PLACES

Because Barney had been a teacher all his working life, he knew how to study a sequence of ideas or actions and work out how to teach them. He thought about the physiology of dancing and realised that the heel step in the foxtrot could be used to help him learn to walk with more control. The heel step grabs the surface with the heel and pulls the leg forward from the hip, rather than pushing off from the heel behind. It meant he was using his thigh muscles, which worked, rather than his calf muscles which didn't. And then he got the idea he could try this running. If he could run, he could take off and land on his feet.

It was at this time, only three months after the accident, that he sent an email to his flying friends: 'I just managed to do 4 x 10 metre dashes! I can only keep going as far as I can hold my breath, as I have to clench my body core against jolting my back. It was very flat-footed, but I was getting both feet off the ground at once and taking long strides and making reasonable speed. I think I'm going to win this battle! Save me a spot on the launch in three to four months!'

He told me later that in reality his 'reasonable speed' was a brisk walking pace and that he only went the length of the veranda, where he could grab the railing if he overbalanced. Without the use of his ankle muscles, the slightest movement sideways meant he would fall over. He also said that he had to psych himself up to imagine the action exactly and then to use all his strength and willpower to do it, as every step created a spasm of agony through his entire body. It happened every time, even though he was still on a full dosage of gabapentin for nerve pain. But it led him to imagine, for the first time since the accident, that he might fly again, like a phoenix reborn.

I don't imagine he thought about the phoenix, burning and

then rising from the ashes, it's not the way he thinks. To me, the point about the phoenix is not so much that it's reborn, but that it actually burns itself. No-one does anything *to* it. It collects the sticks itself, aromatic branches of cinnamon and sandalwood, it sets them alight with one clap of its wings and it stands within the flames and is consumed by fire of its own will. It willingly faces death. It expects to be reborn, that's the storyline; it will be young and powerful again, its sapphire eyes glowing, its red and purple wings glinting in the sunlight. But still, facing annihilation is a high price to pay. What if the story doesn't unfold the way you think it will?

It's the point in my brother's story that I find extraordinary. That he was willing to pay that price again, to step out again into the fiery air – and without any mythic promise that he would arise glorious from the ashes. That he would arise at all.

Sometimes Barney sat quietly in the evening on the veranda, looking out towards Wollumbin, the cloud-catcher, looming in the distance. If the day had not been too hard and the pain had eased, the feeling formed in him that he could walk, run, even dance, like he used to. He could jog in the early morning, he could spring up to catch a ball, or leap over a log, or run down the steps without having to think about it. He stayed as still as he could when this feeling crept over him, because if he moved, the illusion would be shattered.

He kept up the walking and running training every day, some days doing too much and finding he could do nothing the next day. The weariness would overwhelm him at times, but he was getting used to the mental and emotional pattern of it. He reminded himself to use the days when he had the energy to build up his strength and control, and not to berate himself too much on the days he could barely get out of bed. He had never been someone who could do nothing, so he set himself small household tasks to take care of on the days he was too weary to train. He could paint a stool and he could make the wooden louvres for the windows Jenny had wanted him to install for ages. And then the next day he could attempt the four kilometre walk again. And a short run.

At the beginning of March, not quite six months after the accident, Barney decided to start training on specific flying skills. Again, he applied his methodical teaching brain to the task. First he started walking short distances carrying the 22-kilo pack containing his glider and equipment. It felt heavier than it had before and the straps pressed into his thin shoulders, but he expected that. Then he added setting up and packing up the glider in the backyard. It should have been simple but the constant bending and squatting to unfold, spread and refold the wing was exhausting and painful. The fact that he couldn't adjust his ankles meant every action had to be thought through carefully so that he didn't tumble ignominiously over from a squat.

One bright blue windless day in late March, he pulled on his hiking boots and strapped on his flight pack and walked down to Knox Park, just over a kilometre away. There, on a flat playing field, he unpacked the glider, laid it out, checked all the lines and buckled on his harness. It was the same harness the paramedics had cut from him in September the previous year. He'd had it restitched and it was as good as new.

The leaves on a gum tree on the edge of the field moved slightly. Just a faint movement, but he waited anyway. Now they were still. He attached the risers to the carabiners and stood there, feeling the strangeness and the familiarity of the harness and the wing lying behind him. Then he pulled on the A risers, letting air into the cells at the front of the wing. He felt the tug and the gentle lift. He looked over his shoulder, checking that the lines hadn't tangled. The wing rose quietly, a red curve, like a new species of giant mono-winged red butterfly coming to life as air breathed into it. It rose above his head and he pulled on the C risers to prevent the wing sailing over in front of him, but he wasn't quick enough and the wing lifted him. It was just a few centimetres above the ground and only for about a metre, but he still had to land. His feet touched the ground but he couldn't feel it and with little control over his lower legs and none over his ankles, one of his ankles rolled and he fell on one knee. Pain jolted through him. He could feel his heart thumping harder than it should.

He unbuckled the wing, stood up and rearranged the lines and risers, then buckled into the harness again. He checked that the leaves on the gums were still, then pulled on the A risers – the wing rose again; he pulled on the C risers – he was lifted slightly again and he focused on the strength of his thighs and a slight bend in his knees. He landed again, if you could call it that from only a few centimetres up, with both feet straight on the ground.

He kept practising his kiting and ground-handling that day and for weeks afterwards. He had to imagine and rehearse the landing over and over. It wasn't even a matter of not crashing again. Even if he just landed heavily and at an awkward angle, he knew he would undo all the progress he had made in the last six months. His freshly knitted bones and the pins in his spine could break apart and he would be back in that world of agony with no guarantee he would come out of it walking the second time.

He knew falling out of the sky once didn't give him immunity from it happening again. The Fates don't care anything for paying your dues, nor the power of positive thinking. Only the laws of probability: there was as much chance that he would fall out of the sky every time he left the earth. Every time.

# The Rosetta Stone

*Le Puy-en-Velay to Figeac, France*

I have a folder containing all my walking notebooks. The notebooks are all small, but not exactly the same size, and different colours – black, orange, green, light blue, brown – a few are hard-backed, the others are soft moleskin. They are all a bit dirty and tattered, with the odd page torn out. Inside the back covers of each are necessary phone numbers and internet codes – recorded in code – and inside the front covers is written the year and the start and end-point of the walk.

Apart from walking around Uluru, I've kept very few notes of walking in Australia. When I walk in my homeland it's mostly day walks and they don't seem to require note-taking. Most weekends in the cooler seasons, we head out walking in the national parks near Sydney, or in the Blue Mountains and the Snowy Mountains, but not usually overnight, not day-after-day walking. There's little accommodation along walks in the bush and I don't want to carry a tent and stove, bedding, food. I do it sometimes, but I like the feeling of unimpeded walking, of not being burdened with all the necessities of life. Most of my walking has been in Europe, for that reason.

In Europe, and in France in particular, there are low-cost communal *refugios* or *gites* where walkers can stay overnight. Sometimes it's a small cabin with a fireplace, a kitchen, a dormitory, perhaps a tin of lentils left for a meal; other times it's a well-equipped *gite* with dinner provided by the owner. French is the only other language in which I can find my way, which makes France's network of long trails known as *Grande Randonnée* or GRs appealing. I can read the guidebooks, which give detailed notes of the walks in French, and can ask directions when the signs are confusing.

It was pure chance that our walk along the GR 65, the year after walking in Spain, ended in the small town of Figeac on the other side of France's Massif Central. Fated, you could say. I'd had no idea until I arrived there that it was the birthplace of Champollion, one of my childhood heroes. We had decided to finish at Figeac because it was 260 kilometres from the starting point in Le Puy-en-Velay, making it a possible destination to achieve in two weeks. We walked further than that of course, because we lost the way a few times, even on the first day. That day it was in some part due to jet lag – Anthony and I had arrived in France only the day before – but it was also a failure to notice that the signs had changed.

Time and space had seemed stretchy even before we arrived. The flight from Australia, high above places I'll never get to, was as eternal as always. I turned on my flight map in the interminable night to see Mt Ararat and Baku and the Caspian Sea, and, even in my stiff weariness, felt a yearning pleasure in the mysteriousness of the world below. Once we had landed, the train from

## The Rosetta Stone

Paris took hours longer than scheduled after a storm brought trees down on the rail line. It was raining in Le Puy-en-Velay when we arrived and everyone – the 'inn-keeper', shopkeepers, waiters, passing strangers – wore doublets and stockings and velvet gowns. A horde of young men ran by pushing and pulling a metal dragon with a pot of fire under it that shot flames and sparks in the darkness. Banners in the street proclaimed it was the annual *Fête du Roi de l'Oiseau*, the Feast of the Bird King, celebrated since 1524. In the rain and dark and my spaced-out state, it felt as if I had fallen into a time warp.

Next morning, the cobblestones gleamed in the narrow alleys as we crept out into a dark medieval-looking dawn. Le Puy-en-Velay is in the volcanic region of the Massif Central – it has a chapel and a large statue of the Virgin, each built on its own volcanic plug – and as I left the town I kept looking back to admire the drama of the monuments against a blue sky scudding with clouds. The path was quiet, leading through grassy meadows and occasional oak and birch forests. Even though it was September, late autumn, there were flowers everywhere: white yarrow, marguerites, blue harebells, faded cornflowers, dandelions, milkwort. I still liked to make lists in my head as I walked: plants, kinds of buildings, uses of walking poles, reasons for stops when walking, locations of signs, people I met, things remarked on when walking, surfaces underfoot. It was a pointless, absorbing activity, which was probably why I didn't notice the signs change colour.

We followed the red-and-white GR 65 signs, painted on posts, trees, telecom boxes, rocks, sides of buildings, anything at hand. The signs are easy to read: short horizontal red and white stripes for 'continue on', a horizontal red stripe with a white right-angle for 'turn here', and an adamant red cross for 'wrong way'. At a certain point, which I didn't notice – and neither did Anthony – we switched to following the yellow signs used to indicate local walks. We dreamily continued for several kilometres, not bothering to check the GR 65 guidebook.

When Anthony did check, he noticed the description in the book didn't quite match the landscape as well as it might, until we finally realised we had been following yellow signs for we didn't know how long.

'We have to go back until we find the GR signs,' he said.

I was fatigued by then and afternoon jet lag was settling. I could have closed my eyes and gone to sleep standing up, but stoically turned around and followed the directions back until we saw red and white stripes on a fencepost. It was another tired, irritable hour to the *gite* in the village of Montbonnet.

That night I read back over the directions to find where I had stopped paying attention, and realised the walk notes described another location altogether – another set of fields and hills and roads – and yet we had followed them to the right destination. The instructions, in relation to our actual location, were fictional.

'It's a sign,' said Anthony.

'A sign of what? We don't need a guidebook 'cos we'll get there anyway?'

I thought about that for a while. I like following signs – there's a certain reassuring pleasure in it. And it's disturbing or even frightening when there are no signs. How do you know you are going the right way? When I walk, the flash of red and white on a tree is all I need. For Barney there are no painted signs – it's a matter of reading the signs by their effects; a circling bird can mean a thermal, a cloud-street of small cumulus clouds means a run of thermals. That's a riskier business; the signs could always be misread.

I suppose there's a bit of the medieval mind in me – the hope that the world is a book I merely need to learn how to read. Practically speaking, it *is* a type of book: a circle of flattened grass can be read as 'a cat has been sleeping here'; boot prints reveal someone has been this way before and I am perhaps safer than I was. But I can't help reading metaphysically as well: a magpie carolling on a desperate day means there is still hope and beauty; a crow on a fence is a warning. The red and white signs along the walking track reiterate a simple message: in this place and at this time, there is a way. All I have to do is follow the signs. It makes life easy for a while.

The next day took us further into the wild volcanic country of the Massif Central. It was formed 60 million years ago when the African and European tectonic plates collided in that unimaginably dramatic way continents did in those days. The European plate slipped under the African plate, creating the fault lines that caused volcanic activity 25 million years ago. There are 450 extinct volcanoes in the Massif Central, and in the area where we walked, a chain of volcanic plugs or domes called *puys*, which became extinct – or at least dormant – only ten thousand years ago. They created a dramatic landscape of rock domes, some of them rounded, others more like the thick column on which the chapel at Le Puy-en-Velay is so theatrically built. The high limestone plateau is also cut with deep ravines – *causses* – and was dangerous and difficult to cross until late twentieth century motorways pushed through.

# The JOY of HIGH PLACES

The path was littered with silvery mica schist and pinkish sandstone dotted with feldspar, and there were blocky black flows of igneous rock jutting down above us. Everywhere there was a story of a violent distant past, a landscape that showed its bare rocky bones, schist and granite and gneiss, each rock muttering of a saga that had lasted for eons. The villages and farmhouses and ruined chateaux were built of the same rocks and were so much part of the landscape they seemed another geological formation.

Near the end of the second day, I stood in a tiny twelfth-century chapel at Rochegude, next to its ruined castle, once the home of the lords of Montlaur, and felt like I was in a cave. The curved Romanesque ceiling made a dome above me and I could nearly touch either wall if I stretched out my arms; it was as if I were within the rock, in the belly of the earth, even though I was on a crag far above a deep gorge. I walked out of the chapel and climbed down into the gorge, stepping like a goat into the narrow depths. The next morning there was a 500-metre climb upwards, a steep rise through wreaths of mist with a view at the top over to the chapel and the mountainous country beyond. The lords and ladies of Montlaur floated like wraiths in my mind.

Later that morning Anthony and I followed a hand-painted sign leaning on farm machinery, indicating a *buvette*, a small bar. It had been a hard struggle up the side of the gorge and the thought of a coffee had us both stepping along an unpromising cow-shit spattered track past more machinery, until we spotted in an open barn a trestle table with a few cups on it. I stuck my head in the doorway and saw a man in a wheelchair behind the trestle, and behind him, a small coffee machine. There were a few empty plastic chairs scattered about.

## The Rosetta Stone

'*Vous vendez le café?*' I asked uncertainly.

'*Oui*,' he said, and, swivelling his chair, grabbed one of the stained cups, swivelled again, and started making the coffee. He was around 70, overweight, roughly shaven and roughly dressed. I asked if there was a toilet I could use and he indicated a room that had been added inside the barn. I went in and saw that it was his bathroom, with a wheelchair accessible toilet and shower, and a damp towel and clothes lying about.

'You live here?' I asked when I came out.

'Yes,' he said.

We talked in French for a while as he slowly swivelled back and forth from the table to the coffee machine, to the fridge, to the sink. He was so far from anywhere. At the top of a wild gorge, only a muddy track in across the plateau. He couldn't walk anywhere, but he could drive. He made a little income making a few coffees for walkers; no-one else came here. I didn't ask why he was in a wheelchair, what had happened to him. I thought of my brother and his determination to walk again. It could easily have been him, here in this shed. Sometimes determination is not enough, the facts of the body will defeat you.

'*Un sorte de Calvaire*,' he said. A kind of Calvary. It sounded melodramatic to my Australian ears, but I knew it just meant 'it's bloody hard' and was probably an understatement. I wondered how many people followed his clumsy falling-down sign and found his coffee shed; the man who couldn't walk serving coffee to people who walked for fun.

In the evening after we had arrived at the *gite*, showered off the sweaty dust of the day, and found a glass of red wine, Anthony read aloud from *The Way of the World* by Nicholas Bouvier. Bouvier and a friend had set out to drive a small broken-down Fiat from Belgrade to Turkey, Iran and India. On the side of the car they had painted a poem by Hafiz, a Persian poet:

> Even if your night's shelter is uncertain
> And your goal is still far away
> Know that there doesn't exist
> A road without an end –
> Don't be sad.

In the beginning of the book, Bouvier writes that as a boy he had 'stretched out on a rug, silently contemplating the atlas, and that makes one want to travel'. Oh yes, the chant of names in an atlas: Venice, Istanbul, Samarkand, Tashkent … Maps spread the world out into a flat surface that can be read; they transform the world into symbols and signs you can carry around in your pocket. Perhaps the earliest signs and marks made by humans were maps: the lines of rivers, the shape of hills, an impassable swamp, the warnings about bears and wolves, each impressed with a stick on mud or clay.

Bouvier's words flowed in the air, heightening the senses. He journeyed across the Middle East before I was born, yet he brought me into the present and into remembrance of times past. I remembered what I had seen that day, the old stone *lavoirs* for washing clothes and sheets, the *métier à ferrer les boeufs* to hold oxen while they are being reshod, and *cabanes*, which are tiny wheeled wooden houses for shepherds. The constructions reminded me of childhood – the *lavoirs* like the old cement basins we used to rinse sheets, the *métier à ferrier les boeufs* like the four-posted contraption my father used to support birthing cows.

## The Rosetta Stone

I thought often about my childhood farm as I walked, I suppose because we were walking through rough-and-ready farming country like the country where I'd grown up. There had been pretty woods at first – trembling-leafed birches, grey-green lichens, red domed mushrooms – patterned with soft fields and stone fences. But then we were on the moors: dry tough grasses, heather, rocks, upland marshes – bleak and exhilarating. There was a sense of a rougher life, the grass whitened by wind and sun and cold, shaggy cattle, farm-houses made of volcanic rocks, ragged crops of corn for fodder; and along the path, and often in fields, wild broom taking over. It was in this region that the Beast of Gévaudan roamed in the mid-eighteenth century, killing around a hundred people. At the time it was believed to be a gigantic wolf-dog, but today it's thought it was more likely to have been an escaped lion. I looked at a drawing on a sign near a chapel and later saw a statue on a rocky hill, and was struck both times by the fearsome mythical image: its large mouth and teeth, its overly-long muscled body. It was an image of the fearful unknown that could leap out at you without warning and destroy you utterly.

The paw-prints of the beast must have inspired terror whenever they appeared. They were larger than any other dog or wolf prints, and deeper too, and local peasants would have recognised it was an alien print immediately. I've always liked prints of every kind. Growing up on the farm, I could identify the footprints of each animal in the dust before I could read: a horse, a mob of sheep, a singular cow, many chooks, a dog, a cat, a turkey, a snake, lizards, a kangaroo. Prints let me know what is nearby, but I don't think that's the only reason I like them. The tracks my younger son once made in the snow in Paris, the hoofprints of horses on a forest trail in Galicia, the hieroglyphics of magpie claws on wet mud; they each move me to silence, make me feel tender. I'm drawn, too, to the imprint of bodies on the world, not just footsteps. Sometimes, after Anthony has got out of bed, I roll over and lie where his body has lain, press into his body imprint. When I travel, I have put my hand on tombs of saints or walls of grottoes not out of faith, but to touch where hundreds of thousands of other hands have smoothed rough rock into shiny stone. My palm to their palms.

When I first read about the Laetoli footprints, the fossilised prints of three Australopithecus hominids who went walking on volcanic ash 3.6 million years ago, I felt the same mysterious heart connection. The Australopithecus walkers were not in any danger, the volcano was distant, but it had recently rained and made the ash damp. Even now, the speckling of raindrops can be seen on the fossilised ash. And the footprints of three hominids walking, the one behind putting her foot into the tread of the one in front, but not quite exactly, and another one, smaller, perhaps a child, walking beside them.

At one point they paused and turned to the left before continuing on in the same direction.

The sun soon dried the damp ash, which hardened and set the footprints forever. Millions of years later, Mary Leakey's team of paleoanthropologists found them in the Great Rift Valley in Tanzania. The footprints they found under the sand – first an animal print, then 70 humanoid prints – became the earliest direct evidence that our ancestors did walk upright. I thought of long-ago ancestors out strolling, one behind the other, pausing to check something out: a bird flapping away, or perhaps to discuss which way to go now – towards that hill to the left or

## The Rosetta Stone

straight ahead? It's the pause, the turn and then the heading on that gets to me.

It was the same when I saw images of the Mungo footprints, found by a Mutthi Mutthi woman, Mary Pappen Jr, in Australia in 2003. One cool Pleistocene day, 20 000 years ago, a family – adults, teenagers, a small child – walked across the wet claypans of Lake Mungo. Shortly afterwards sand blew into the footprints and preserved their shape as they dried out. The clay contained calcium carbonate, which hardened like concrete as it dried so the distinct prints are exactly as they were the day the family walked across the claypan. There are in fact 700 footprints at Lake Mungo, imprinted at different times, including a group of five hunters, running very fast, mud squeezing between their toes, and even a one-legged man hopping expertly, but it's the small child who feels familiar. She paused, ran back in the opposite direction to everyone else, perhaps picked up a feather, a stick, then turned and walked back quickly.

The tracks have been studied by archaeologists and by local Indigenous men and women. It didn't take Pintupi trackers long to see the imprint of a man standing with a spear, the line of a spear being thrown, and where a woman had moved a baby from one hip to the other. They knew how to read the signs.

When I first heard about both the Laetoli and the Mungo footprints, I immediately wanted to go and see them, but soon found out that both sets had been re-covered with sand to protect them, not just from vandals, but from the weather. I can gaze at photographs or models, but it's not the same. I wanted to look at the real tracks – and, I admit, I wanted to touch them. I wouldn't put my feet in their footprints, but like a devout pilgrim, touch them with my hands. Just very gently with my fingertips: fingertips on the footprint of a child who lived 20 000 years ago; a child who lived three and a half million years ago.

And then I wondered if claw-prints and foot-prints inspired the first writing? Did we humans get the idea of writing from seeing a natural record of what had happened, imprinted in mud? The run of small hoof prints behind larger prints, the snake track in the dust, the crisscrossing of ibis tracks like a manuscript gone crazy, each patterning the clay by the stream – didn't each one tell a clearly readable story? It would not have been so much of a leap to one day gather and flatten and smooth some clay from the same stream into a tablet and press shapes into it – a toe-print, a stick, a stone – and then show your brother.

'What do you think this means?' you ask.

'It means you walked by the trees and up the stony hill,' he answers.

'Yes,' you say, 'that's what it means'. And writing, a maze of signs pointing at all of reality – more than that, making reality spring into mind – came into being that day.


The upland was an isolated place, even now. The plateau was over 1830 metres high and the people who lived there did not see the need to come down to the lowlands very often. It was late September and there was an autumnal chill, a sense of the world retracting for the winter ahead. I wore several layers, felt the cold air on my cheeks, and felt somehow at home. I mostly walked in silence, but every now and then I remarked or pointed with my walking pole at various things which, after a while, fell into categories of 'things remarked upon': types of crops, breed of cows (Highland cattle, from Scotland), types of rocks, the kinds and shapes of trees, the colour of soils, types of gates and fences, farm machinery, the beauty of the morning, anything that reminded me of something in a book.

At Domaine du Sauvage, where we stayed in a huge thirteenth-century hospital founded by the Templars, I was seated at dinner next to Kenji, a young Japanese man. In fact, I only thought he was young – reading his face and his sweet uncertain manner, I placed him in his twenties, but he told me he was nearly 40. He showed me, and then others at the table, his book of drawings in pencil and black ink. He didn't take photographs or write notes, but sketched what he saw. The neatness and precision of his drawings reminded me of Barney's paintings, the exact recording of a world. There were fine architectural drawings of barns and crucifixes, and detailed botanical observations: rose hips, spear thistle, burdock; and sketches of creatures: the friendly black dog we had also met, a horse peering over a stone wall, bees, cattle.

What I saw in his book was his walk, the things he 'remarked' upon, what attracted his attention and moved him to take up his pencil or his ink pen. I was looking through his eyes, walking in him. It was a finer journey than mine, more detailed. He said he walked slowly, stopped often, watched. 'It will take me a long time,' he said.

In Saint-Alban-sur-Limagnole the next night, I had a radio interview from Australia to talk about a book I'd recently written. I stood in the cold and deep silence behind the church, holding my phone high, trying to find and keep a signal from the other side of the world. I was tired and couldn't find the words. That night I dreamed that one of my sisters had died; and then, a few nights later, I dreamed of Michelle, a friend who had died a few years ago. I didn't know what to make of the dreams. The surreal stories of dreams are hard to read, like trying to read hieroglyphics without the Rosetta Stone. The images of death shimmered under the day, a kind of palimpsest of shadowy night images of motherless children beneath bright daytime scenes: eating apples in fields, sun on my face, deep dappled pathways through twisted beech forests. It felt as if the walking was making me more susceptible to impression, as if I were becoming clay.

On the eighth day, the path descended 500 metres into the Lot Valley, leaving the moors behind. Anthony and I walked down through mottled light in beech forests and on stone-walled paths so old they had been worn metres below the level of fields. The country down here was warm and soft; the beeches gave way to oaks and chestnuts and the coarse moor grasslands were replaced by green meadows. On the side of the path grew yarrow and mint, dandelions and nettles, blackberries, blueberries and aloes. It looked like a land of plenty.

But things were not what they seemed. In Belvezet we stopped at a stone barn where an elderly couple were serving coffee and orange juice, for a euro each, to walkers. More of the villagers came out, all of them elderly; I have a photograph of them coming to the barn on their sticks, like elderly children of Hamelin emerging from the cave at last, eager for company. I thanked the old woman and she said, 'I don't have to go and see the world; the whole world comes to see us'. Yes, I thought, that's good, but soon these villages will be empty. The young people have already gone and the old people are lonely and will die soon enough. Only the villages that can sell their beauty and attract tourists will survive.

In Conques a few days later, there were shops selling

trinkets, and plenty of cafes and thousands of visitors, but nowhere to buy vegetables, fruit, meat, or groceries. The countryside all around was so beautiful it easily exhausted my adjectives – in fact, I simply wrote 'bliss' in my notebook – but the town had become a museum of itself. It had a cathedral with a stone carving of the Last Judgment above the main door, with the writhing damned on one side and the joyful saved on the other. There was also an abbey church built in the eleventh century, famous because it holds the remains of Sainte Foy, who was tortured to death by the Romans in the third century. The bones were kept in her hometown, Agen, but a thieving monk made off with the bones and brought them to Conques.

I realise it's the stories of wild beasts and saints' bones imprinted in the landscape like a kind of strange dark lace that kept me walking as much as the landscape itself. I could read these stories in stone: I grew up with the idea of the damned and the saved, they echoed back to the child sitting in a church in the bush, looking up at the crucifix and plaster saints. I was a pilgrim, but not a holy one.

I did see a holy pilgrim on the day we walked out of Conques. At least I thought he was one at first. The climb out of the valley was long and steep, not my favourite geography first thing in the morning. My calves were painful, stiff after a couple of days rest in Conques. I kept stopping and standing backwards on the hillside to give my muscles a break. I felt irritable. Despite the exhilaration of walking, a contradictory part of me hated making any physical effort, but I tried to hide it. At one point Anthony said, '*Retrouvez votre sérénité*'. Chill out.

'Don't tell me how I should be', I snapped.

'No,' he said mildly. 'It was written on that post there.' He pointed with his walking pole to a small neat sign that I'd missed.

I laughed. 'Okay, I'll take advice from a post.'

It was a few hours later that I saw the pilgrim. I was traversing a rocky hillside – Anthony was 50 metres or so ahead of me – and when I stopped and turned for a moment, I saw a man striding up behind me. He was lean, tanned, fit and wore nothing except a sort of kilt and boots and had a number of religious medals glinting on his bare chest. I was surprised by the medals – no-one else I'd seen wore any obvious religious images – but more by his nakedness – men just do not go about bare-chested in France. I didn't think anything of it until he said something to me in French just as he was passing. I didn't quite catch it, and asked what he said. He stopped on the rock above me and said it again, but again I didn't catch it. But then he opened his kilt as if to adjust the tie or clip at the waist, just enough to reveal his genitals and said, and I caught what he said this time, *'Est-ce que cela vous gêne?'* Does this embarrass you?

*'Non,'* I said, *'pas du tout'*. I even had the presence of mind to add, *'Il fait chaud'*. No, not at all, it's hot weather.

Anthony, just ahead, hadn't seen a thing. 'I've just been flashed,' I said, as I caught up. We both laughed. It seemed an extraordinary length to go to, walking hundreds of kilometres just to reveal his sexual organs to an occasional walker. We named him the Pilgrim Flasher, but didn't see him again until a couple of mornings later. I was eating breakfast at the *gite* where we'd stayed the night, when I realised the man sitting next to me was wearing the same kilt. I quietly ate my yoghurt and tartine.

# The Rosetta Stone

It was October now and the last day of walking. Anthony sang as we walked though grassy meadows and oak-lined lanes. It was an old Leonard Cohen song, 'Bird on a Wire'. It was one of the songs he used to sing to our boys when it was his turn to put them to bed. I've always loved it when Anthony sings, especially when he sings as he walks; it gives me a glimpse of his soul. All that can be seen is a man, now in his sixties, not tall, with thinning hair, walking easily, but anyone listening could read the dreaming young rebel who lived inside him. *He has tried in his way to be free.* It's strange how much of life cannot be seen and has to be read in small fragments that sometimes surface. Perhaps everything simply exists and there is nothing to read in any of it, but I can only imagine such a pure state of being. I don't know what decoder I am using, but I know I am doing it all day, every day.

It was only a short day, 11 kilometres, into Figeac, which the walking notebook said had *'charmantes rues médiévales'* – charming medieval streets – and an abbey church consecrated in 1093. We followed the railway line in until we came to a sign saying *Place des Écritures*.

'Place of Writings,' I translated aloud. 'We have to follow that sign!'

We abandoned the red and white GR signs and followed the tourist signposts along cobbled streets and alleys until we came to another sign announcing the *Musée des Écritures* and a tiny square, enclosed on all four sides by walls, more a large courtyard than a square. At one end there were archways and columns and behind them a cloister. Around the walls there was an outdoor exhibition of paintings of bees.

'It's all about you,' Anthony said. The book that I had talked about in the dark street in Saint-Alban-sur-Limagnole had bees on the cover. It was enough synchronicity to encourage the illusion of a speaking world. It doesn't take much.

I looked down at the unusual smooth black basalt paving and saw that it was engraved with some sort of writing and hieroglyphs. With a sudden delighted shock I realised I was standing on an oversized facsimile of the Rosetta Stone. As a child walking over the farm looking for fossils and bones, I'd loved the Rosetta Stone; it was the transforming key to ancient mysteries accidentally found lying in the desert by an ordinary soldier. For me, its discovery meant that treasure could be found anywhere at any time; that all you had to do was step off the track you were following, and if you kept a sharp lookout, and if you were very lucky, you might find something. In the trackless wilds, the caves and rocks and creeks might have been hiding something for eons. For all the reassurance of following signs, I've always known there's a wild pleasure in random revelation, the thing that will only be found when there are no tracks to follow in the unmapped wilderness.

The Museum of Writing, I soon discovered, was devoted to Jean-François Champollion, Figeac's most famous son and my primary school hero; the first person to decode the Rosetta Stone. He had studied ancient languages from boyhood – Greek, Hebrew, Syrian, Aramaic and Coptic – and after years of working from drawings – the English wouldn't allow him to see the original engraving – he finally translated the Rosetta Stone in 1822.

The stone had waited quietly for 2000 years, a broken stele of granodiorite, an igneous rock made of quartz and plagioclase feldspar – a type of rock also found on the moon and on Mars

## The Rosetta Stone

– a pleasing if irrelevant piece of information. In 1799, a French soldier, Pierre-François Bouchard, found the stone, some say in sand, others say in a wall near the town of Rosetta, about 70 kilometres north of Alexandria. There were three scripts on it: hieroglyphics, Greek, and demotic Egyptian – which Champollion deduced was very like Coptic. From the Greek it was easy to read that this was a decree issued by Ptolemy V in 196 BC, stating that statues should be erected in his honour in all temples and that celebrations should be held. More significantly, it also said that the decree be inscribed in hieroglyphic, demotic Egyptian and Greek letters – in other words, it said: this is the same thing written three times.

It took Champollion's painstaking study to work out that the hieroglyphs were in fact mainly phonetic, that they were letters rather than pictures, and then, letter by letter, he deduced the value of each hieroglyph. With that, the whole written language of ancient Egypt could be read and the long-ago past revealed. Champollion showed that the Egyptians had in fact invented phonetic writing. The Egyptians themselves, however, had given the credit to Thoth, their ibis-headed bird-god.

It's curious the way the world seems to pattern itself, as if it truly does want to be read. I know it's not a book written by God, but surely it could not be human to regard a flat impermeable world, a world that simply exists. Who alive can resist the desire to find meaning in the rhythmic repetition of images, in the return of the moon, the claw-prints of magpies, the shape of a heart in a rock. It's what we do.

I stood in the courtyard with bees on the wall and the Rosetta Stone underfoot, my pack still on my back, boots dusty. For the moment, the 16 days of walking seemed to have led me to where

I needed to be. Then, today I looked again in the small black walking notebook for Le Puy-en-Velay to Figeac to see that I'd written just one day later, 'Restlessness now. Where to go? What to do?'

# Phoenix rises

I keep thinking about not being able to walk across the top of the cliff around Mont Blanc. I had the chance to face and overcome fear but it paralysed me, turned my legs to water, made me physically unable to walk. It was much more difficult to deal with than physical pain – in fact, for me, impossible. Each time I imagined walking over the path, thinking, I will see myself do it and then I'll be okay, the fear rose again, making every part of me unable to act. I imagined being on the other side of the death-walk, and yes, there I was, but immediately afterwards came the image of the steps I would have to take on that icy slope above the chasm and the fear surged back like a wild drug. I had to crawl away from the edge on all fours. No longer a walking woman.

This fear makes it difficult for me to imagine how Barney could decide to fly again. Each time my mind tries to imagine it, each time I try to put myself in his place, my body rebels. It's too easy to die. For the story to end. To understand at all, I have to rely on the detailed answers he sends to my questions. When did you decide to fly again? Were your friends and Jenny okay with that? How did you feel in the weeks and days leading up to it?

Didn't your body rebel? I send questions every few days, feeling more and more like a species of voyeur. I wondered how close, how far inside someone else, I was allowed to be.

'I'm ready to fly again now,' Barney had announced. It was near the beginning of May the year after he fell when he told Jenny his decision. He had completed two months of practice, now he would wait for the first day when all the conditions were right: sunny with one or two small clouds, and a light breeze, around 15 kilometres per hour. He felt excited and nervous once he had made the commitment aloud. Jenny was anxious, but according to him, she said, 'You were so much happier once you began flying. I'd rather you take the risk again and be happy.' I asked her directly when I saw her at Byron Bay around that time – I met them there several times – and she said much the same thing, but I could see the shadow in her eyes. He wrote to me later, 'There was really no alternative for me. Flying is an integral part of who I am, I couldn't live and not do it.'

Two weeks after he made the announcement, Sunday 20th May, the perfect conditions arrived. He checked with the Bureau of Meteorology website and the wind station at the launch site. These days there's also a webcam on the cafe across from the site so it's easy to check the weather in real time from home, but the weather report was enough to reassure him on that day. He emailed his flying friends to let them know he was driving up to Beechmont, the same hill he had launched from last spring, eight months before. As he drove through the farmland and native bush towards the launch site, the nervousness that had been building took hold of him. His stomach clenched and he suddenly felt dizzy. What if he couldn't do it? What if he had to walk away in front of all his friends? There was too much to lose – everything he had gained in the last eight months. He was lucky to be able to walk. He could just turn around now and go home. He blinked hard and hauled his mind back to driving the car, concentrating on the road in front of him.

And then he was on the hill and his friends were greeting him. It was a gentle blue day and everyone was happy to see him. He could feel their warmth and encouragement, and their fear for him. Was he a kind of superstitious offering, making them all safe? There were a few tourists too, standing near their cars further up the hill, waiting for someone, anyone, to start flying. His heart was much louder than it should be, so loud surely his friends could hear it. His stomach swirled and he felt as if he might throw up. He took small sips of water and rolled his shoulders to loosen them. Jenny stood nearby and smiled, but he could see the worry in her eyes. He looked at the sky; the small cumulus clouds that might have some uplift under them, weak but smooth. He looked at the trees. Just a faint movement of leaves. The grass was browner than it had been in September. A long hot summer and a dry autumn had passed without him noticing.

Everyone was waiting. The day was perfect for flying. He had unpacked the wing, checked it, attached and checked his instruments. There was nothing else to do. He clipped into the harness, looped the bungy under his heel, clipped the chest strap shut and then pulled his gloves on. He gathered the wing up and walked the few steps to the launching area.

Everyone was watching. Gavin helped spread the wing behind him. It was painful bending and squatting and easy to become unbalanced. He didn't want to tumble sideways from a squat in front of everyone. Then the wing was ready. His hands gripped the brakes.

He pulled down on the A risers and felt the wing tug on his shoulders as it lifted and ballooned. He let it rise over his head, a shadowy red sun lifting above him, then pulled a little on the C risers. His stomach was settling now that he had to concentrate. He turned and walked forward, his hands still firmly gripping the brakes. He released the risers and the wing surged forward a little; he picked up his pace, loosened the brakes and then he lifted lightly and easily off the ground, just like in his dreams.

There were loud cheers and whoops and clapping behind him. The whole world was relieved and happy. A surge of joyful exhilaration coursed through him and he felt as if his whole body must be shining. A smile split open his face and his eyes pricked with tears. His legs were tucked into the flying pod, his arms were strong, his wing obeyed his every adjustment. He was free and light, floating, untrammelled by anything.

He flew higher, gliding in a ridge lift, then found a small thermal that let him soar a few hundred metres above the small figures waiting on the hill below. The ranges were below him, the sky above, he was in a 360-degree world that extended forever. He felt the cool fresh air on his face. It was a beautiful May morning. He was a skinny, dark-haired child again, bursting with joy. He was above the farm, Mum and Dad were there near the house, standing in the backyard and they looked up and saw him flying above the chook yard and the wheat paddock. Like an angel, they would have thought, filled with golden light.

He wasn't thinking anything. There was just the sensation of the wing above him, lifting and dipping with the air currents, and the pull of his arm muscles responding to the shifts, and the feeling that he was breathing right to the edge of himself. He didn't believe in souls, but he was living right up to, over the edge of, his skin. There were no eagles today, no wild soaring thousands of feet above the earth, but it didn't matter, the fabled door to joy had swung open again.

And then it was time to face the demon. It never had been taking off, or flying. It was landing. He couldn't stay here forever. From the moment he stepped off into infinity, he had always had to come back to earth.

'I have to attempt a landing,' he told himself aloud. Attempt. He couldn't alert the awful Fates by saying anything more certain than that. He was going to try to land on the 'bomb-out', the same place he had hurtled to earth eight months ago.

As he flew over the landing site, he could see the wind sock was at a low angle in the direction of his approach, indicating a head-wind of around 15 kilometres per hour. Even though it looked safe, he circled over the site once, checking his ground speed, then circled back for his final approach. He noted the still leaves of the gum trees below on either side of the landing site, and the still grass beneath him.

His heart was beating absurdly loud again, his stomach turning over. Nerves thrummed, tightened, clamped. His instinct, as always as he lost height, was to pull on the breaks, but it was crucial to maintain airspeed because below the height of the gum trees there was sure to be a wind-shadow, and without sufficient speed, the drop into the still air could cause a stall. The wing would deflate and he would be in freefall.

He flew at trim speed with the brakes up and just enough pressure to feel any feedback from the wing, any turbulence or change in air pressure. He flew below the level of the gum trees and into the wind-shadow, maintaining his speed. The ground was rushing towards him very quickly now, his feet skimming over the grass. It was late autumn kangaroo grass, creamy and long, moving under his boots. He was as close to landing as he had been eight months ago.

He concentrated on the ground beneath him and on the delicate shifts in tension in the wing above him. It was an extension of his nerves, his sinews and muscles. It was part of him. He pulled slowly and smoothly down on the brakes causing the wing to slowly flare, just like a bird flaring its wings before it lands.

Then he landed softly, his feet hitting the ground without a stumble, and the wing sank gracefully behind him. There was a jolt of nerve pain, 'the usual' he said, and then a sensational flood of confidence. He grasped the lines in one hand and pulled on them and the wing bunched into a rosette that he could hold steady against any gusts of wind. He was standing upright, on the ground, in one piece.

He had fallen and been broken and then, after all that, he had leapt off the earth and flown through the sky and had known himself to be at home there, and then returned to the same place where he had fallen. He waved to Jenny and to the other small cheering figures standing on the hill, then he unstrapped his harness, shrugged out of it and put it on the ground. He calmly and methodically began to gather the wing so that it could be folded and packed, ready for next time.

# Becoming wild

*Carcassonne to St-Jean-Pied-de-Port, France*

It's hard to go on after triumph, perhaps even harder than going on after despair or loss. After cataclysm, if you don't die you must go on; but after triumph there should be nothing more to do, the story should happily end. No more complications. But of course it doesn't work that way. You have to keep getting up, taking action, taking risks. You have to deal with daily life. What do you do next?

What I did next was to walk. Again.

For some time I'd wanted to walk further, much further, than before. We had walked up to 300 kilometres at a time, but now that didn't seem far enough. I don't think it was just addiction, the need for a larger hit, although it easily could have been. It was more that I had begun to believe that if I kept walking, every day, day after day, for weeks and weeks, something would change. What that something was I had no idea, but I wanted to find out. Perhaps it would change my mind? Or my heart? Perhaps I'd be cured of restlessness.

I could see it was the same for Barney, the desire to not just keep flying, but to fly higher and further and across unexplored country; although for him, it possibly wasn't to do with restlessness. When I tried to pin him down, he didn't mention being restless but kept returning to the idea of *being himself* when he flew. As I try to pin it down now, it keeps slipping away, but I want to say it's something to do with a sense in both of us – I want to claim in all of us – of yearning that is assuaged, and perhaps only momentarily assuaged, by becoming free, untrammelled in the landscape or skyscape, moving through earth, air, fire, water. It's an old, old longing that won't leave us alone. It gets us up in the morning after all joys and sorrows; it keeps us going day after day. It might even save us.

Then one son, the one who keeps his old backpack even though it is torn and dirty, gave Anthony and me a book, *A History of the World in 500 Walks*. It had photographs and short descriptions of each walk that made me realise again the impossibility of knowing the world. I read the book and made lists of possible walks, and then narrowed it down to walks we could do in a month. Around 500 kilometres. Then I narrowed it again to walks that had somewhere to sleep at night along the way so we didn't have to carry our world on our backs. I bought the Topoguide book for the *Grande Randonnée 78*, which runs from Carcassonne in the south-east of France to St-Jean-Pied-de-Port in the Pyrénées, most of the way from the Mediterranean to the Atlantic.

# Becoming wild

On the evening before we started to walk, four men stood up in front of the altar in St Nazaire basilica in Carcassonne and began to sing. There was no announcement, they simply opened their mouths and out came glory. The songs, from the Russian orthodox liturgy I later read, had a deep solemnity that made an unidentified receptor under my heart ache. It felt as if a membrane stretching there had waited for this sound forever, but now that it had heard it, it was not soothed because the sound awakened endless yearning. The men were barrel-chested, with deep voices, born in the ribbed caves inside them, effortlessly flooding the basilica. They sounded like the Russian and Georgian buskers I've heard in the Paris Métro filling the tunnels with infinite longing; echoing, echoing. Even when I rushed past with a busy, empty head in the corridors of Châtelet or Bastille, I could feel their voices stretching my ribs as the longing hit and expanded.

The singing felt like a random gift at the beginning, like a talisman, but it was unsettling to be back in Carcassonne. Anthony and I had come here with our boys more than ten years ago, when we were living and working in Paris. They were grown young men then, but still single. I had felt such love for them, and some sadness, sensing that this would be the last time we were together before they fell in love with others. I remember the week we stayed in that cold stone house near Carcassonne we all read Louis de Bernières' *Captain Corelli's Mandolin*, which, at the end, jumps forward many decades. I remember hating the leap forward to a time when the lovely young ones were old. Why didn't the writer leave them in the time of endless love and youth?

Next morning I waited on the Pont Vieux, the bridge over the Aude where the walk began. I stood for a moment, feeling the pack sitting lightly on my hips, poles in one hand, feet on the cobbles. Anthony took a photograph on his phone. There was a certain anxious determination to my stance; I'd had a virus that wouldn't go away for the ten weeks before – not serious, but wearing – and I had lost fitness and confidence. I had thought I might have to pull out, but then the 'Fuck it, I'm doing it anyway' response had kicked in. A dose of blind, unreasonable determination can come in handy at times. I did my pared-down packing ruthlessly: one change of clothes with extra socks and underpants, sheet bag, small towel, raincoat, a combined sun-block moisturiser, phone, GR 78 Topoguide, compass, notebook and pen.

For the first few hours the path led along the Aude and through the suburbs and villages surrounding Carcassonne. The medieval walled *cité* rose romantically against the sky behind, but ahead the bitumen and concrete footpaths passed suburban homes. The thrill of beginning subsided under the weight of neat fences and gardens and pink-ochre houses. The wriggling worm of 'Why am I doing this?' surfaced briefly, but then came the release of vineyards and sunflower fields on either side of the path.

The vines were heavy with black grapes, just before harvest, and the sunflowers were huge brown-seeded disks, some as large as dinner plates, heads bowed in final obeisance to the sun. The world started opening out to me. I saw a gold and white butterfly with blue points on its wings clinging to a blade of grass in the strong breeze; men collecting small white snails into plastic sacks; stripped wheatfields that reminded me of childhood: straight furrows, yellow stalks, clods of earth. Mint and yarrow grew everywhere along the side of the path. Old fig trees dropped black fruit and I ate the warm figs. There were almond trees too, old and gnarled, but the almonds were too hard to crack, even with the help of a rock.

There was no-one else walking that day, nor the day after, although there were hoofprints, neat horseshoe shapes in the dust, in front of us. At one point the Topoguide instructed *'serpenter au milieu du vignoble'* and so I happily snaked through the middle of the vineyards. Large, tight bunches of grapes begged to be picked and eaten. I gathered a few for lunch and, sitting on a grassy hillside eating bread and grapes, I couldn't help thinking of the Holy Communion of childhood.

In those days I knelt at the altar rail, eyes closed, tongue stuck out, waiting for the round wafer of bread and a sip of wine from the chalice. It was a mystery, the story of the bread and wine being actually the body and blood of Jesus. It didn't make any sense, but I tried to believe it anyway. Transubstantiation, a word I've known since I was seven when I made my first Holy Communion, explained that while it still looked like bread and wine, the miracle of the priest saying words over it had changed it into the 'real presence' of God. It was no wonder my rational brother rebelled at the nonsense of it. And in my turn, so did I. Yet now, I love the far-fetched nature of the narrative I'd been asked to believe – that a God could be ordinary food and that I could consume Him.

Anthony and I stayed at a convent in Fanjeaux that night, a vast series of rooms inhabited now by only three nuns. An elderly woman served us dinner and breakfast with silent care. Earlier in the afternoon I had seen her acting as a guide in the local thirteenth-century Gothic church that had a display of highly wrought church vestments, woven with gold and silver threads and embroidered with mystical patterns.

# The JOY of HIGH PLACES

Here in this quiet town, the local villagers and nobility in the twelfth and thirteenth centuries had rejected such displays of material riches and, along with it, the power of the Church. They were Cathars, who advocated and practised a return to the simplicity and humility of Jesus, to truly follow in his footsteps. The Church saw this rejection of its authority as heretical and sent St Dominique to gather the villagers back into the fold. The following year, 1207, an oratory 'duel' was arranged between the future saint and the Cathar bishop. At the end, there was a judgment by fire – both men were to throw their words into the flames. As might be predicted in this story, the words of the Cathar bishop were consumed by the flames and St Dominique's flew out of the fire intact and floated to the ceiling.

I read the story out to Anthony as we sat in the convent garden drinking beer out of a thermos. There were more stories from other millennia: in the early first century AD there had been a Roman temple here dedicated to Jupiter; in the fourteenth century the town was burned to the ground by the Black Prince. Did any of the stories mean anything now?

The short Filipina nun who had let us into the convent trotted past, looking curiously at our thermos. Anthony picked up his phone and read aloud from WG Sebald's *The Rings of Saturn*; I had read it before and knew its richness and depth, its flooding darkness. At first it seemed the wrong choice to be a walking companion, with its dissections of decay and horror of every kind, but soon it became clear that it was weaving a necessary dark thread in the bright physical day of walking. The sun was hot in the convent garden, there were roses and bees and butterflies, and Sebald was leading me into the blackness of colonialism in the Belgian Congo.

## Becoming wild

As we walked out early the next morning, light caught a plane tree and transformed it. Behind it was a petrol station and, beyond that, the town of the Romans and Cathars and St Dominique and the Black Prince was still asleep.

It was the third day of walking and the first day the Pyrénées appeared, as if a painter had just got around to blocking them in. They filled the distant horizon with clear blue lines of jagged peaks all that long day of walking. Their clarity reminded me of Barney's paintings, as if they had been created with scientific precision. No moody interpretation here; the splendid facts were enough. The map indicated the mountains were 40 or 50 kilometres away, but they felt like a guiding arm lying across the landscape, shepherding me along.

The path led through more fields of stalky wheat and heavy-headed sunflowers, through shifting coins of light in a birch wood, past stony hamlets and farm machinery and hedgerows, and across a meadow where the path was delineated by looped wire to stop us tramping all over the farmer's pasture. Along the hedgerows, orange and black butterflies rose as Anthony walked ahead of me and, beneath my boots, the horse's hooves clip-clopped their exact journey. I began to look out for her prints – I thought from the beginning she was a mare – noting where she had picked her way down a slope, and where she slipped sideways a little in the mud as she came up out of a stream. The morning sun touched lightly. I felt a blossoming warmth arise in my chest and flow out into my limbs.

'I think I know how to walk at last,' I said.

'It's the morning bliss,' said Anthony.

We had both been walking long enough to know the pattern. The first two hours were blissful, body and soul glowing;

the second few hours were solid accomplishment; the last two or three shifted between silent endurance and snappy irritation. There was no point in being romantic about it. All the same, my body was finding its strength after the weeks of illness: back straightened, leg muscles stretched, arm muscles strengthening with each pull of the walking poles.

A week into walking, the horse's hoofprints disappeared. After the market town of Pamiers, the path became steeper and rougher and I wondered if the horse's journey had ended because it was too tough, or whether it had kept going but we were too far behind now and the prints had disappeared. We were swerving southwards into the foothills of the Pyrénées; it was going to be hard walking from now on. I had pasted an altitude profile of the whole 500 kilometres into my notebook before I left home and most of the profile looked like a child's drawing of dramatically spiky mountains.

Between Pamiers and Montégut-Plantaurel there were two peaks marked. The path became narrower, steeper, rockier, up through chestnuts, beeches, oaks, robinia, then beeches again, and then pines and firs with green mossy feet. Legs stretched upwards, arms pushed down on the poles, balanced, reached the next rock, stretched up again. I was beginning to feel like some sort of mountain creature: a goat, or even a monkey. The day was hot and I had to drink water often. When I stopped to pee, I dug a hole with the heel of my boot and covered it over afterwards, cat-like. Only disturbed earth and leaf litter was left.

And then the serried, snow-covered peaks of the Pyrénées appeared again, brilliant white with deep blue shadows, and stopped me in my tracks. I realised the peaks we had seen on the third day were only the first rung of the mountains, a mere hint of the fierce country beyond. We were much closer now. The snowy peaks glittered dramatically against the sky like a postcard image, but I knew about mountains. Mont Blanc had taught me respect. It felt as if I were re-meeting a beautiful friend who had made me afraid.

The path had turned southwards, heading towards the range, but in the next valley the peaks disappeared again. I found myself longing for them each time I climbed upwards, the brief glimpse, the reward, before the path plunged down again. Then in another few hours, stretching and struggling upwards, rounding the curve of the slope and there they were again, another glimpse. It was like walking a labyrinth, coming close to the source, to being able, nearly, to touch beauty, and then being swung away again, losing sight of it altogether, way out on the edge, remembering only that there once had been a moment of revelation.

I thought about writing during this day and the next days as the path kept heading south and the mountains were closer, clearer with each glimpse. Before I left I had been working every day on setting down my brother's stories. He had already given me everything I needed, answered every question in fine detail, shown me not just a bird's-eye view, but a bird knowledge of air and wind and clouds. I saw hawks often as I walked, and an eagle once, and each time I thought of him. How his shoulder and chest muscles must stretch, how he had overcome a natural human inclination to keep his feet on the ground, and how none of his skill or methodical nature saved him from the random havoc of a small whirlwind. The hawks circled above high meadows and woods in their domed 360-degree world, in which I was of less interest than a field mouse and in no way necessary.

Days became harder and longer. The swing southwards had taken the path into the Hautes-Pyrénées region, up over passes, descending into deep ravines and scrambling back up again. On the twelfth day, as we walked towards Juzet-d'Izaut, the path at one point was so narrow I could only put one foot in front of the other. It traversed a long slope above the tree line, so steep that any misstep would have meant a fall of more than 100 metres. It was longer than the Mont Blanc crossing that had defeated me, but without slippery snow it was a 'possible' rather than a certain-death. I didn't look down or up; the whole world contained no more than the path in front of me.

Later on, stands of Pyrénéen oaks towered, grand and silent. I didn't hear or see any animals in the forest, although the horse's hoofprints had appeared again. As soon as I saw the prints there was a surge of fellow feeling. She had kept on going. Of course there was no reason to think it was the same horse, but I couldn't help attributing continuity – an ongoing story – to the reappearance of the prints. Each time there was a difficult traverse or a muddy slope, I looked out for her prints to see how she had fared. Did her hooves slip sideways, did she go around the fallen branch or over it, had she slipped on the slate, did she find another path up through the rocks?

I had ridden horses as a child on the farm and often rode bareback. I was skilled and courageous enough to gallop headlong across the paddocks, although it wasn't to last. I remembered the 11-year-old girl I had been, her physical toughness. I knew then the feel of a horse under me as it scrambled upwards; the stretch and rhythm of the legs, shoulders, haunches; the sweaty smell; the wiry mane; the clamp of my own legs over the belly. And then slowing down, cantering across the paddock in the sun, wind in my chopped hair, knees locked into the movement of the horse's gait.

It was still hot and our water bottles ran low. There wasn't a lot of potable water along the track, or at least not marked as potable, and so from the first days of walking I had stopped at barns, knocked on doors, called over fences, asking strangers to fill our bottles. Each time it was need that forced me to ask, but each time it was oddly as if I had done something for them. The woman at an isolated auberge, three hippies in a barn, two men building a shed, a group of men and women out mushrooming, a man sleeping on a couch in the heat of the afternoon whom I woke with my knock; each time they delighted in being able to help. And as I drank, so I peed like a cat, in woods and fields, by the side of the path, behind trees, out in the open. In the upland meadows, short chestnut horses with wild blond manes galloped towards the fences when I stopped to pee, lifted their heads and watched. I thought how simple life can be.

That night we stayed with a couple, Julie and Jean-Pierre, who ran a private *gite* in their home. Julie had her hands bandaged and her face held the strain and aging of long illness and pain – I thought she was Jean-Pierre's mother at first. They were religious, a fact made obvious by the bottles of Lourdes water in the shape of the Virgin Mary by each bed, as well as an atmosphere of resistance to change I recognised from childhood. As I knew from my earliest years, the Virgin had appeared to a young girl at Lourdes and told her that the water was healing, and since then it had become a centre of pilgrimage for millions of the faithful. I asked Julie if she had been to Lourdes.

'Of course,' she said. 'Many times.' And then she told me about her illness, an autoimmune disease that was attacking and breaking down her flesh. It was most severe in her bandaged hands but most of her body was in pain most of the time. Jean-Pierre looked after the house, cooked for her, cut her food up as if she were a baby. She told me that she smoked marijuana for the pain. Ah, that accounted for the familiar smell I'd noticed when I was coming down the stairs and had discounted in this religious household. I stifled the impulse to say it was probably of more use than the Lourdes water.

On the thirteenth day we headed towards St-Bertrand-de-Comminges, which, the Topoguide, said was 'suspended between the earth and sky'. A whole town floating. Like my brother, I thought, floating above the planet. What is it about human beings that we keep devising ways to feel weightless, to be beyond the earth, to be winged, to be suspended? When I asked my brother what he thought it was, he had given me the 'mastery' answer; that all our efforts came from the pleasure of extending our capacities. He may be right, but I wondered if it was more to do with the common enough desire to escape our bodies, to become untethered. It's the subject of so much poetry and a part of religious experience, that desire to burst free of the body into communion with everything else. It has always been there.

I plodded along – there was too much bitumen road walking that day, which is dispiriting in itself as well as making knees and hips sore – and then up and over a long rocky mountain. My palms were sweaty on the walking poles and I couldn't look up for fear of losing my footing. Still, the strange stillness that fell just before noon each day on the countryside arrived in silence, and quietness flowed into my body. The noonday hush, I suddenly realised.

I bought local sheep's cheese, hard sausage and small tomatoes at a farmer's stall and we sat by the Garonne River and ate them for lunch. Afterwards, I took my boots off as usual and lay by the river in the shade and ate windfall figs. That night in St-Bertrand we ate at a restaurant that only served one meal, the same meal for everyone: soup, salad, confit and fruit, prepared and served by one man, cook and waiter on his own. The next night, at Montsérié, there was no shop and no restaurant and we were offered two tins of food by the mayor, who had opened the *gite* for us. Lentils and sausages in one tin, Mexican salad in the other. The following night, in Esparros, the shop was closed for the season, not opening until next summer, but I saw a man gardening and asked to buy some tomatoes to go with the dried pasta we'd been offered. He complained about the weather, and gave me four tomatoes and wouldn't accept payment. Each day it was a relief not to have to choose what to eat. This was all there was, this is what we ate. It was a paring down to what was essential. Asking for water, asking for food. And walking.

There's a photograph of me by the Garonne, after I had my boots back on, and there's a loose air of confidence about me. I felt strong and ready to continue on through the long afternoon. I remember thinking I could feel the 11-year-old girl inside me, wiry and unselfconscious. I was my body, sore here and there, muscled, sweaty; and my body fitted the landscape. I felt like a cicada uncrumpling its wings in the sunlight after a long time in its chrysalis under the ground. It might have been the beginning of a shift that day, the change I had been hoping for without knowing what it was.

# The JOY of HIGH PLACES

On day 16, we walked towards Escaladieu, translated as 'ladder to God', and saw a white crane and a brown eagle above the chestnut and birch forest. The river Arros flowed beside us, the round stones in its bed shining in the clear water. Deep blue crocuses filled small clearings. Later there was a bright red fungi in the shape of a starfish on the side of the path, a sea creature on the floor of the dim woods, and just out of the forest there were two yellow-eyed goats staring at us with evil intent. I saw my horse's hooves had sunk deep in the mud where cows had trampled along a lane. A tidy woman who reminded me of Jenny, Barney's wife, filled my water bottles at her kitchen sink in a farmhouse. Days had slowed down to intense moments without purpose, without needing to be read. Days had become simple.

In the middle of another forest a text arrived from my younger son, the one who gave us the *500 Walks* book, with a video of his one-year-old daughter taking her first steps, and I watched it over and over. I couldn't stop smiling at the delight and pride shining in her face as she walked upright from the kitchen and across the hall and then sat down, overcome with her accomplishment. Today she had stood upright and headed out across the world for the very first time, staggering a little, but pleased that she had joined the two-legged ones.

From Escaladieu to Bagnères-de-Bigorre and from there to Ourdis-Cotdousson there were several steep climbs, one of them over 1100 metres. Each time, there was a resistance to the effort required, the stretch of calf and thigh muscles, facing back down the mountain to stretch muscles the other way, clambering across streams on bridges made of fallen trees, stops for water, scrambling over rocks, sure-footed, sweating in the autumn heat, then finally reaching the top. The joy of high places sang through my body. I was a winged creature. There in front of us was the astonishing beauty of the Pyrénées, the peaks ranging back into infinity in patterns of light and shadow, and I felt the physical pleasure of a body extended and a kind of pride in having endured.

I've been trying to remember the details of the sensation at the top of mountains, but they slip away and all I have are the brief notes I took in the evenings. Then I wonder why I want to re-create the joy of high places, or in fact any of the experience of walking. It can never be what actually happened, no matter how many details I recall. When it happens, it's in the body, the muscles and joints and cells; and in the brain, the thousands of neural pathways firing with electricity, somehow constructing the shock of beauty and pleasure along with a self who experiences it all. Then there is a feeling of lightness filling the chest cavity and a joyful sensation floods through the cells of the body. I know people who are religious call this a spiritual experience, but I think it's human. It ought to be enough that it happens.

On the nineteenth day we walked into Lourdes. The journey took longer than expected as we both missed a GR sign. I don't know why Anthony missed it, but I was gazing southwards, to the left of the track, trying to imprint the Pyrénées in my memory. I had seen them many times by now, rising as I climbed upwards, and disappearing as I descended into the valleys, but this time I was traversing the side of a hill that gave a balcony view of the serried ranges, dreaming back in shades of blue. It was photographically perfect, the exact image of mountainous beauty I had seen in books as a child, the pleasure of perfect verisimilitude, but there was a physical sensation that I don't think any representation could convey. There was a startling clarity and then a sense of being in this landscape, of being an element in it. I was not apart from it, an observer looking at a view, but immersed in it, part of it. I came to the end of the balcony road, and realised I hadn't seen a sign since I didn't know when. Neither had Anthony.

We decided to walk onwards down the hill towards a village – the impulse is always to go forward – but no signs appeared. Neither of us were sure where we were so the guidebook instructions didn't help. We finally faced the fact that we had to go back up the hill, back along the road of astounding views, this time looking for signs instead of beauty.

We clambered up a long hill and along a ridge for a few kilometres, then scrambled down the long slate-covered slope of the Pic du Jer, through prickly bushes, until we reached the city where the Mother of God had appeared in a small cave on a rocky hillside.

In Lourdes in 1858, Bernadette, a pretty, dark-eyed teenage girl came home from gathering firewood and said she had seen a 'a small maiden' who spoke to her in a cave. She appeared several times, then, Bernadette said, she declared herself to be Our Lady of the Immaculate Conception, the Mother of God. This was when she told Bernadette to dig in the ground at a certain spot where the spring with healing properties bubbled up. At first the young girl was ridiculed, but when miraculous cures were reported she was believed, not just by the townspeople, but by the officials of the Church; and the pilgrims began arriving. Even now, in the twenty-first century, over five million people visit the shrine every year.

Who knows what Bernadette saw, or what was happening in her mind, but this was a familiar story for me, a familiar place with familiar furnishings: statues of saints, rosary beads, candles, holy water; objects which were perfectly normal in my childhood in the scrub on the other side of the world. I felt a fond detachment looking at it all. I was an unbeliever, but also recognised that I felt at home.

I walked up to the grotto in the valley of the Gave de Pau River, surrounded by three high peaks, the slopes on three sides creating a feeling of enclosure and protection. It had been raining the morning after we arrived, but now it was clearing and a few others had ventured out into the damp grey afternoon. A queue had formed at the grotto, moving slowly and peacefully into the dimness and coming out the other side. Above the grotto was a veiled statue of the Virgin Mary. I joined the queue while Anthony waited.

As I entered the cave opening, the young, dark-haired, olive-skinned man in front of me placed his palm on the rock, and then I saw that everyone else was doing the same. In fact, the rock had been worn as smooth and shiny as marble from millions of hands doing the same for more than 150 years. The touching of holy places was not part of the Irish Catholicism I grew up with, but I put my hand out too, laid my palm flat on the rock. None of it, the prayers and candles and the Virgin Mary, were part of my story any more, but I understood this, the laying of hands on ancient cave walls. Touching the earth was like cupping a child's cheek, or holding one of my stones; for a moment I was at one. The overhanging wall was slightly warm, oiled and darkened by sweat, the roughness of the rock worn smooth.

I thought about Barney and how, even in the depths of pain, he had not resorted to our childhood faith or in belief in miracles of any kind. He used reason, trained his mind. I hadn't even realised he was in pain most of the time until one evening when I was having dinner in Byron Bay with him and Jenny. It was a noisy, busy cafe in the main street with windows opened to the buskers playing outside. Barney sat quietly like he always did, not saying a lot, while Jenny told me about their trip to Europe. Barney said he couldn't walk far when they were sight-seeing because of the pain. I was surprised. It was a couple of years since the accident and he hadn't talked about pain for a long time.

'Are you still in pain sometimes?' I asked.

'I'm always in pain,' he said. It sounds melodramatic but it was the most matter-of-fact statement you could imagine. The fact that there was no asking for sympathy or any sense of drama in his tone was just as shocking as the fact that I had been totally unaware of his pain.

'What do you do about it? How do you manage?' My ignorance made me uncomfortable.

'I concentrate on the parts of my body that are not hurting. Early on, that was only my hands. Or that was what it seemed. It was hard to tell where the pain was coming from.'

'So it was, is, all over your body?'

'Not now. It's mostly just my feet and legs now. Before, it was everything from mid-torso down. In the first few days there was this weird 360-degree sphere of pain around my legs. It was like my brain didn't know where my legs were because of the damaged nerves, so it gave the range of every possible place my legs could be in pain.'

I don't think I had ever been so aware of how much of other people's experience escapes me. Why hadn't I noticed something as vast as a 'sphere of pain', or at least its aftermath? I had read his silences for far too long as lack of interest, getting his story entirely wrong.

In Lourdes I walked around the grassy valley outside the grotto, and along the river, looking at the stands of candles, the flickering flames and the twisted forms of melted wax. Touching earth, watching fire. I thought about my father and how much he wanted to believe in God in His heaven; to know, with his whole heart, that He was there. The air was fresh and cool, the sun had broken through and calm enveloped the valley. For me the earth was enough.

It was still cloudy but not raining next morning, the beginning of the fourth week of walking. The first signpost said *Grotte du Loup*, the cave of the wolf, and the path led along the Gave du Pau through a Pyrénéen oak forest. I'd read there were a few wolves in the eastern Pyrénées now, and once on that day I did see a set of paw-prints in the mud that were much bigger than any dog-print I'd ever seen, but it wasn't likely to have been a wolf that far west. I thought about my horse-companion and how she would have reared up in terror if she'd seen one. Her hoofprints continued on steadily, now on a path that was veering away from the mountains and was not quite as steep and rocky. In the woods, the forestry track was knee-deep in sticky clay-mud, churned in places to a metre deep by heavy logging trucks and tractors. I struggled, clambering along the edges of the quagmire for nearly a kilometre, trying not to fall in. Afterwards, in the 'cow alleys' between fields, wet green cow shit mixed with the mud. Mud spattered up my trouser legs as far as the thighs and then onto my face as I swung my poles around after heaving them forcibly out of the wet clay.

The next day when the sun came out it was hot whenever there was no shade, but the mud continued. By the following morning, the choice of clothes was muddy or muddier, but it didn't matter. I remember standing in a dappled clearing – I had stopped for a coffee from the thermos and then a pee behind a log and I was ready to go again. It was day 24 or 25, I had lost count. I stood with both poles in one hand, dried mud pale on the bottom of my pants. I looked at my arms and saw on each inner arm near the elbow, a new muscle, or at least one that hadn't ever appeared before. Every muscle felt hard and working the way it should, there was a lithe sway to my body, the sweat had dried on my skin; I could walk forever; I could ask for what I needed – water, food, directions – and someone would give them to me. I felt pleasure in my dirtiness and in my unbrushed red hair, and in not needing anything else. I would go where I wanted, when I wanted. I would look after myself and other people would offer me whatever leftovers they could. Feral, I thought, a wild creature gone bush.

'I do know how to walk,' I said.

'Yes,' said Anthony. 'It takes a while.'

The path wound on easily and allowed the mind-floating that comes on long walks when you don't have to concentrate on keeping upright. It can't be called thinking; it's not that distinct and probably is nearer to dreaming. The French philosopher

Frédéric Gros said, 'There is a moment when you walk several hours that you are only a body walking. Only that. You are nobody. You have no future. You are only a body walking.'

I remembered the question on the boulders on the Lairig Ghru walk. 'Why are you out here?' If such things were said aloud, and if I'd had a surer footing on the boulders at the time, that's what I might have said to the three young men when they asked what I was doing out here. I am only a body walking.

I suspect it is the same for Barney. That when he flies, he is only a body flying. And even though flying is only possible because of modern aerodynamic physics and technology, it seems more primal than walking, more fundamental. The dreams of sleeping children flying through the sky above farms and towns and oceans – does every human have such dreams? – tells me the longing is not constructed, it is seeded deep within us. Under all our wars and cruelties, inequalities and pettiness, it would seem there is the longing to fly, to be at one with the elements. My brother is in the sky with his eagle eyes, finding the thermals and cloud-streets and letting the wind stream through his wings.

I thought about people helping us along the way. Giving directions, filling our water bottles and thermos. Making us meals, giving us shelter. We had relied on them, especially for water. Every day we had to depend on strangers. We had become vulnerable. And then I understood that vulnerability connected us to others and saw for the first time that making myself independent, self-reliant, 'strong', actually distanced me from others. Why had I spent so much time doing it? Vulnerability is our shared condition.

The path led out of the forest, through meadows of wet grass and then open fields of stripped sunflowers and then, on the

# The JOY of HIGH PLACES

way to Oloron-Sainte-Marie, I thought about writing. Mostly I thought about what is selected to write about, and what is left out; the usual impossibility of including every thing, every moment, the multiplicity of the texture of being. I want to put the whole world on the page, all the sights and sounds I've left out of my notebook: a bull in a meadow regarding us with solemn disinterest; the church bells that rang every half hour through the night, keeping me awake; the palest salty yellow of sheep's cheese; the hot air balloon that rose outside the early morning window in Escaladieu; the laundromat day in Lourdes; listening to Janis Joplin in a cafe one night with my 16-year-old heart stretching beyond itself; a spider's web with dew jewels glittering on it; a snarling dog just as we came out of a beech forest, the low terrifying sound of it and the red-black of its inside lip.

Do I need to say everything? James Joyce said, 'Any object, intensely regarded, may be a gate of access to the incomprehensible aeon of the Gods'. Maybe just one thing, any object, is enough.

However much truth is told, most of it is left out. There's just not enough time to tell it all; how can anyone ever say what happened, even in one day? Even in one minute. I could start a list in my head: bootlaces need tightening, my palms are sweaty on the walking poles, there is mint and yarrow all along the road, Anthony is 50 metres ahead of me, one hip is sore, the path is heading upwards into a cool birch forest, a hawk circles, an image of my brother chatting to eagles flits into my head, I'm hungry, there's a cool breeze on my face. And, because I'm thinking about all of it, mirrors reflecting to infinity form in my mind. I know that when I write I am trying to do something impossible. Sometimes that thought hurts the inside of my ribs, but today it doesn't matter too much.

# Becoming wild

The walking is not difficult now, although there are steep hills to climb. There are two or three days to go, to L'Hôpital-Saint-Blaise and then to Mauléon-Licharre, and maybe further if there's time and if knee and hip joints hold up. I am not sure which day it will finish, but I know for certain I will be sad for days afterwards. Whenever I finish, however far I walk, I know it will feel as if I must keep walking. I keep believing that one day, one day, I will start to walk and continue walking until the end of my life. But today the sun is shining and I've reached a birch wood and there are drifts of leaves underfoot. I start singing. I'm not much of a singer, but I was in a choir once, so I sing every fragment of every song I can remember. I walk and sing for hours.

# A short walk home

*Suntop Church to Baron Rock, Wellington, NSW*

I let my brothers and sisters know I was going up to the farm and Baron Rock. It's something each of us does every now and then, a return to our country. It's not owned by anyone in the family anymore, hasn't been for more than 40 years, but it's still ours in heart and memory, which meant I didn't like having to ask to walk on it. Why should I have to ask to walk through my own heart? It's Wiradjuri land by a much longer story than mine, but I was born there and took my first steps on that soil and all my memories have that earth underneath them and that sky above them.

But I rang Robert Anderson, who was five years old the last time I saw him, and asked him if I could walk on Marylands, the old farm. I explained I was Don Miller's daughter. 'No worries,' he said.

Then I rang Owen Johns who owns Baron Rock, to ask him if I could walk across his back paddocks to the Rock.

'I've got some ewes lambing in the back paddock,' he said.

# A short walk home

'I'll be careful of them,' I said. There was a short silence. Even when I explained I'd grown up there, he sounded a bit puzzled.

'It's pretty dry and bare there at the moment.'

'That's fine,' I said. 'It was a drought most of my childhood. I'm used to it.'

I agreed to send him a text when I arrived, just so he would know I was there.

Anthony drove up to Wellington with me the night before and we went to the Lion of Waterloo for a drink. It's the oldest pub in Wellington, built in 1842, about the time my ancestors first arrived there. The last time I had been to the Lion was for the wake after my mother's funeral five years before and the pub had been packed with her descendants and their families; eight children, about 25 grandchildren and countless great-grandchildren. The winter night had vibrated with sadness and lost children. Tonight it was full of footballers happily celebrating their afternoon game with their families and supporters; young mothers carried babies and kids ran up and down on the bricked veranda dodging the drinkers spilling out the door.

Anthony read aloud, but quietly, from Patrick White's *Voss* and I leaned close to hear. We had been reading it every evening for weeks – he read, I listened – trudging through the outback with the German explorer. Tonight the chapter wasn't about Voss' great and hopeless walk, but the story of the birth of the baby, Mercy, not far from where we live in Sydney now. I sat there in the noise of sporting victory, my eyes filling with tears at the birth of a fictional baby.

# The JOY of HIGH PLACES

The next morning Anthony dropped me off at the old tin church 20 kilometres out of town. It had been our local church, but someone lived there now; they had added a chimney and a dried-out garden. A dog started to bark wildly as I got out of the car. I looked down to see a pale green parakeet lying dead on the yellowing grass. Not great omens, but I shrugged them off; the world was not always here to conduct a personal conversation with me.

'Got enough water?' asked Anthony.

'Yes,' I said. 'See you later. Thanks.' I strapped my backpack on and tightened my laces. I just wanted to start walking. Down from the church, along Bennett's lane to the farm and across the paddocks to the old house, then up to Baron Rock. It was under 11 kilometres there and back, just a morning's walk.

'Shut up, Millie,' someone yelled at the barking dog. I turned away from the church and walked down to Bennett's lane and around the corner past the old mailbox lying on its side on the ground. There was white lettering, D Miller and JO Harris, still visible through the rust; the names of my father and the farmer who lived on the other side of the lane.

It was a bright autumn day, a dome of blue sky overhead; the early morning air was cool. The lane was still dirt, the way it always had been; the same gum trees gathered here and there along the side of it. The slight rise towards Jim Harris' gate, the hard sandy ground underfoot, the sound of cattle mooing uneasily, the small knobs of lucerne in the reddish-brown dry paddocks unfolded all at once into a papery time-tunnel back to the 11-year-old girl walking home from school. Chasing Jenny Bennett with a pig's skull; stalking along in a storm of tears about some hurt I don't recall; collecting shot-gun cartridges at a clay-pigeon shoot on Jim Harris' farm. Flies buzzed around my face and I brushed them away with a continual automatic movement of my hand.

A fox ran out into the lane, thin and lithe, and stopped short. We looked at each other, astonished, then he turned and leapt back over the fence and up the bank of a dried-out dam. Then I was at the top of the last hill, where we often stopped as kids to wait for each other. At the bottom was the gate and the track down to the house. From here I could see Baron Rock against the horizon and, in the middle distance, a clump of gum trees in front of the small smudge of the farmhouse. The paddocks were bare and dry.

I'm home, I thought. Wherever I walk, whatever I do, this is home.

I walked down the hill eagerly, but the gate was no longer there. The fence line running up to it had been shifted, making the layout of the paddocks different, not quite unrecognisable, but disorientating. I climbed over the fence and tried to find the track I had walked on every school morning of childhood. It had disappeared, not even any rutted tyre tracks, but I knew where it was in the soles of my feet. I threaded back and forth across the unfamiliar fence line, following the track up from the creek, which was nothing more than a dry gully, and then passed where the sheep-yards had been. A large mob of sheep milled and eyed me suspiciously just down the slope towards the creek.

There was the house.

I was ready for it. I had seen it a decade before and knew it had been abandoned. Left to the work of weather and time. It was already becoming derelict then – the light blue paint patchy and worn, and the roof rusty – but it had been intact. Now the roof was missing from the back of the house; the outside toilet had a roof but no walls, the toilet pedestal sat white and foolish, open to the world; the mud-hut that had housed the electrical generator had finally dissolved and sunk and was now just a tin roof on a mound of clay. The kitchen chimney had fallen down into a tumble of bricks; one of the water tanks had slid off its stand; sheets of corrugated iron covered what had been the kitchen window. I peered through broken boards into the roofless kitchen and lounge room, cluttered with bits of tin and fibro and boards. How small they were! How could ten people have gathered in these poky rooms? This was where we had all learned to walk on the lino floors, done our homework, argued about who was to do the washing-up. Around the front of the house, the veranda and its roof had slipped off, leaving the walls exposed, ashamed. I wasn't ready for it.

I walked around what had been a garden of sorts at the side and front of the house. The cape honeysuckle which, in those days, had red flowers whose nectar we kids used to suck like strange wingless honeyeater birds, still grew as a harsh stalky bush; and one of the row of feathery Athel trees that Mrs Kelly had given our mother one year had survived. And the large peppertree, blown over in a freak tornado when I was ten, was still alive, lying on its side. And the kurrajong tree. Kurrajongs always survive. But no grass or bushes grew in the hard ground littered with sheep poo.

I long to be able to say how all this affected me; the immensity of the past living inside me, threatening to expand and overflow, and the dissolving melancholy of physical decay, but I can only write down what I saw.

I hadn't meant to go into the house because it looked

dangerous with sharp tin and rotting boards, but I started clambering over the fallen veranda beams and corrugated iron. I wanted to see my bedroom, the one I had shared with Mary. And my parents' room, which opened off ours. And my brothers' sleep-out. The front door was jammed shut but there was a doorway-sized hole into my parents' room, so I stepped carefully in. It was cluttered with an old kitchen dresser, a television, boxes of books, but what knocked the breath out of me was that it still had the green walls and purple ceiling my mother had chosen in the sixties. I hadn't realised the wild colours of those years had reached all the way out to the west and into my mother's quiet, sardonic mind.

I looked in a box of books, all of them hardcovers from over 50 years ago, but I didn't recognise any of them as ours. I looked through into my room. There were chairs by the old fireplace, again not ours, but there was a broken-doored wardrobe that looked familiar, perhaps from the boys' sleep-out, and weirdly, an orange life-jacket. The mantelpiece over the fireplace had disappeared, the floor was covered in ash and dirt so thick the lino wasn't visible, and the grey slab walls were dirty with cobwebs and dust. I looked up at the board ceiling and thought to count the boards. No, I don't have to; I know there are 29 and a half.

I walked into the passageway, always dark, and the boys' sleep-out, where Barney had designed his wooden wings – and kept his end of the room tidy. I thought of him flying over the farm in his dreams, all of us in the shabby house, flying over the farm in the night.

I walked outside and had a swig of water in the shade of the kurrajong. Sheep and lambs baa-ed, a crow cawed, magpies carolled in their absurdly fresh way: the orchestra of my childhood. I wasn't sure what to do. I had intended to walk to Baron Rock – the farmhouse had not been a destination, just a place I was passing by – but seeing it had left me in a vast and tender silence. The past is weighty when it arrives with its full armoury of memory. I didn't want to move.

No, keep walking, I told myself. This is not about walking back into childhood, the place of the eternal present. It's a trap. I am being waylaid by the powerful constructions of the past and they are sapping my energy. Just keep walking.

It was two kilometres to the Rock, past the shearing shed and the collapsed wheat shed, and then over the fence into Owen John's property. Here there was long yellowing wire grass and umbrella and kangaroo and spear grass, a creamy apron dotted with ewes and lambs.

I circled around the sheep as promised, but they still watched me anxiously from the edge of the gully ahead, then scattered away. In the gully I saw a new lamb, which, unaccountably, had its head torn off, and I felt afraid. I had lived for 18 years on the farm and walked all over it and across other farms and had never seen anything like this. Its head was completely gone, just the bloody neck left, although the rest of the body was unmarked. It could have been a wild animal, like the Beast of Gévaudan, I thought, and realised how easily my mind leapt to the fantastical, how little it took to abandon rationality. It must have been a fox.

The Rock loomed above me and then I climbed over the fence and was in the shade of the gum trees, kurrajongs and she-oaks around its base. The ground rose steeply and was scattered with boulders, grey-green with lichen, in front of a sheer rock wall.

# A short walk home

I headed towards the side where the outcrop lengthened into the shape of a crouching animal. I could climb up somewhere along its spine. The ground was dry with only eaten-down knobs of whitened grass clinging here and there among the rocks. A flock of light green parakeets rose, squawking at the disturbance in their domain, and then, as I scrambled over a fallen branch, a kangaroo leapt away in front of me. I looked down and saw a kangaroo path along the side of the slope, a soft, paddled path, not hard and narrow like sheep tracks.

I followed a track under the eucalypts, heading higher all the time until it reached the shoulder of the crouching animal. We started further back as kids, at the back haunches where the rock sank back into the earth, but I reckoned I could climb it easily here. I stopped for a moment and had some more water. The morning had warmed up and I was hot and sweaty already.

I reached up, held on to the rock and hauled myself up. It was steep, but there were plenty of ledges and crevices to hold onto, so that it was more of a scramble than a climb. I reached the rock-pool plateau that I knew was at the top of the shoulder. The rock pools were dried out, as I thought they would be; the moss was blackened with the long summer heat and the grey-green lichens were shrivelled. I knew this place. Its geography was in my head, but more than that, each shift in the surface of the rock underfoot and the grassy smell of the air. I breathed it in.

I continued up along the spine, through the tussocky grasses and small she-oaks clinging onto the rock face. At the summit was a deep crevice with a rock jammed in it to step over before reaching the indented seat formed in the boulder at the very top. There it was, just as I remembered. I slipped off my backpack and sat in the rock seat and let its cool arms enfold me.

It was silent. I had never been here alone before. A small fleet of swallows circled nearby, but no eagles or hawks. I wondered if this was where all our flying dreams were born. Perhaps this was where Barney first realised that he had to be able to fly, where his bird-soul started to form.

I had intended to take some notes as I sat there but it seemed superfluous. I've thought about, written about, this rocky outcrop so many times, I have wondered if I may have invented it for my own use, my own inner temple to hang my soul in, but I have asked my brothers and sisters, and they all feel the same. It's enough that it is there, it doesn't need to be owned. I unpacked my small picnic instead and sat for a while, eating an apple and looking out at the dry landscape.

I stayed for half an hour then headed back down the spine. As I came off the rock and back onto the steep slope, I saw a mob of four kangaroos bound away out of the bush at the base and head towards the west of the Rock. I climbed back over the fence and down towards the gully and home. I remembered I had not greeted the Rock as I arrived so I turned around to yell goodbye, at least.

It didn't answer and, for a moment, I thought, 'It only speaks to children'. But I knew it was a matter of the right distance, the right angle, so I walked another 20 metres, turned around again and yelled 'Goodbye'.

'Bye,' said the Rock, casually. I smiled like a child and turned round and kept on walking.

# Chrysalis

I had been worried about showing Barney the story of how he learned to walk again. It was drawn from the notes he sent me, his answers to my questions, but it still felt as if I had invaded him in some way. I remembered when he was at dinner at my place one day, volunteering some details about flying, how conscious I was of trying to hide my greedy eyes, my greedy mouth. There's always the anxiety that our hungry bloody teeth are showing as we eat other people's stories. But, truthfully, I also worried it might be too confronting for him and that he would realise he didn't want to have his world exposed in that way. Fair enough, why would you? I didn't tell him my constant fear that he might refuse to tell me anything else, but I did warn him that it might be traumatic to read.

'I'll be fine,' he said. 'It's long enough ago now. It won't be a problem. I think I'll be fine.'

I still felt doubtful. I know what happens when things are written down. But I was going up the north coast to visit him in Murwillumbah in a couple of weeks and I couldn't hide it from him any longer. I sent the stories of falling and walking to him, along with the ones about him flying again. I thought maybe the flying again story would balance it out for him, a kind of antidote. I also confessed to my past judgments of him and hoped he would forgive me.

I waited anxiously for a few days. Barney normally answered the same day, or at least the following day. He had realised that none of it was any of my business, I was sure of it, and he was working out how to tell me. I had been expecting it all along. Perhaps he was planning to ring me to tell me to drop it. I wouldn't blame him; I wouldn't want someone else digging around in my life like that.

Then the email came. 'Strange though it might seem, my emotional response to your narrative was way stronger than my response to the actual events at the time,' he wrote.

I knew it. It was always the way. Memory is more powerful than life, and writing is more powerful than memory. Life would be thin, a transparent shadow, without being remade over and over in songs and poems and stories.

And then he went on to say that 'there was no need to be anxious about your remarks about me. I know I've always been a bit reserved about my inner thoughts and emotions and I realise that most people who know me only get to see a fairly superficial picture of who I am. I've opened up more as a result of the accident and the support shown to me by so many people.' There was more about his feelings, about how he knew he had operated on a 'need to know' basis emotionally, and that people from different parts of his life – flying, teaching, dancing – wouldn't recognise each other's version of him. I sat there reading, overwhelmed. I felt as if I were meeting my brother for the first time.

After a neat paragraph break, he changed topic to describe a flight he'd made the day before from Mt Tambourine, how he had been flying at about 6000 feet and it was freezing. He had been so cold he was shivering uncontrollably and was worried hypothermia could set in, so instead of flying on he set down in a landing paddock nearby. Then he added, he had put a painting in the local Rotary art show and had won first prize.

Anthony and I drove north to Byron Bay a couple of weeks later. As we drove, I thought about whether I could fly or not. The thought had flitted around the edges of my mind ever since I'd started writing Barney's story. It didn't pull me in the same way that walking did, but I knew that was partly fear. I gazed out at the coastal rainforest and paddocks and then sugar cane fields, feeling, as always, that I'd arrived in another country.

I met up with my younger brother Kevin at the Bangalow markets. He was the comic of the family and told me how much fun he and Barney had laughing together. 'What a great sense of humour Barney has!' he said. Again, I felt the small jarring that happens when a new piece of the picture has to fit in. It was another thing I didn't know about Barney.

The next afternoon we drove through the rainforest in the Nightcap National Park, pulled on our walking boots and walked the 13 kilometres to Minyon Falls and back. Tall tallowwoods and blackbutts and strangler figs towered around us, making the bright blue winter day dim and greenish. On the last morning of our trip, we drove to Murwillumbah, about an hour north of Byron Bay, to have lunch with Barney and Jenny. I had my notebook in my bag.

# The JOY of HIGH PLACES

When I stepped out of the car, Barney was waiting across the road on the grassy footpath. We hugged as we met and then, when we got to the top of the steps of his Queenslander, he stopped and smiled. It was a welcoming smile, transforming his thin face, but it also had another quality to it, an extraordinary openness. I smiled in return. We knew each other now.

Jenny was inside preparing lunch in the pristine kitchen. We greeted her and then Barney announced he was going down to the park to show me how the paraglider worked. I realised when we got there it was the same park he had been practising in for months before he flew again. He hauled out the paraglider backpack and asked me to carry it so that I could feel its weight.

'How heavy is it?' I asked as I shrugged it on.

He grinned as I staggered a bit under the weight of it. I was used to carrying no more than six kilos, even on the longest walks.

'When I have the water and all the gear in it, it's around 22 kilos, but it's not that much at the moment.'

I carried it over to the centre of the park – it was a playing field, but there was no-one else about – and put it down. Barney pulled the wing and the harness out and lay them on the grass, a complicated mess of strings looking as if it would take hours to untangle. He put the harness on his back, clipped up the various belts and methodically attached carabiners just as he had described in his careful explanations.

What he had not told me was the strange effect of the pod of the harness dangling behind him, as if it were part of his body. It was attached to one foot with a loop so that when he flew he could swing it up and put both his legs in it, but at the moment, the pod hung behind him and dragged a little on the ground, like the thorax of a giant insect, so that he looked like a cicada, halfway out of its nymph shell or a butterfly almost out of its chrysalis. He moved about, concentrating on clipping the carabiners and tossing the wing expertly to untangle the risers, unconscious of his metamorphosis into a large flying creature.

'I told you about the eagle attacking me, didn't I? See where it tore holes,' he said, holding up the leading edge of the wing. The sets of four holes where the talons had pierced the fabric were neatly patched. I could see the eagle flapping and screeching, attacking the intruder in its territory. It could easily have collapsed his wing or mauled his face.

Then Barney took out a white mask made of a heavy cloth; calico, I think. There were hemmed square holes in it for eyes and mouth and hemmed slits above the ears for his sunglasses, but other than that it covered his whole face and neck. He had made it himself to give protection from wind, cold and sunburn when he was high in the thin atmosphere. He was good at sewing – when he was a teacher he used to make all the outfits for his classes at school concerts, sewing 60 leotards at a time. He pulled the mask on, and his sunglasses and helmet, and suddenly looked extremely bizarre.

'It scares the kids when I land in their paddocks,' Barney said.

'It would scare me,' I said.

'And then I breathe like this,' he said, doing the long slow Darth Vader breathing. We both laughed. I had somehow thought of Barney as being outside of popular culture, that he wouldn't know about anything that had happened in films and music in all the decades since we were children.

'How often do you do this?' I asked.

# The JOY of HIGH PLACES

'Flying? Three or four times a week if the conditions are good.' He spread part of the wing out. 'Would you get that corner and spread it for me?'

'Sure. Wow! You really fly that often?' I knew it would take up most of the day each time he flew, driving to the launch site, flying, landing and having to hitch-hike back unless Jenny or one of his flying mates were handy to pick him up. In all this time, I had not realised how much of his life was centred on flying. Most of his life. I had thought it was something he did every few weeks.

I ran and spread both corners of the wings then watched, fascinated, as my insect-brother walked forward with his chrysalis dragging behind him, tugging on the C risers and letting the air fill the cells of the wing. It lifted instantly, gracefully, billowing overhead. Barney ran, and I ran to keep up with him. It was a flat playing field, no slope, so he only lifted off a few centimetres, but the wing was tugging at him, making him light, ready to leave the ground behind. The unknowable blue sky was opening up in front of my fresh-winged brother.

Afterwards he let me try the harness to test its weight and feel the wing behind me. I put on the mask and helmet as well, and became the insect-woman. I could feel my thorax and chrysalis against the back of my legs. One day perhaps I would fly. Not alone – the skills and strength required years of practice – but one day with Barney. It could be possible.

Barney looked at me questioningly. I smiled and shook my head, just a little. Perhaps I hadn't said no.

Later, when we arrived back at the house, he hung the

harness on hooks in his shed so the pod formed the seat of a swing. I climbed in, belted up and sat back. I tucked my legs into the pod and stretched luxuriously.

'It's so comfortable,' I said. 'You could read a book while you were flying.'

'Well you could, people do all sorts of things, but you really need to be paying attention.' And he told me about a hang-glider pilot who had been posting photos on Facebook as he flew and had crashed into the wing of a paragliding friend of Barney's, and the two had become entangled. Her wing wrapped right around her – 'she was gift-wrapped', he said – and they both plummeted towards the ground, still wrapped together. The hang-glider pilot was able to release his small emergency 'chute at the last moment and they had landed in a tree, neither of them badly hurt.

'So, no reading books then,' I said.

We went inside as Jenny started to bring the lunch to the table.

'I couldn't get Patti to come and fly with me,' said Barney. We all laughed.

We talked over lunch about our families. Barney and Jenny's adult children were still all living overseas: in Auckland and Dubai, and one had moved to Chiang Mai, so they didn't see them very often. I noticed the sideboard behind was covered with photographs of their son and two daughters and their two grandchildren. 'We take what we can get,' Jenny said. 'And we Skype.'

On the walls there were several large paintings that Barney had done. There was one seascape of rock pools with a sea-eagle flapping in just above the rock platform and another of a field with a mountain in the background, both of them photographically exact. 'Contemporary realism, I'm told,' Barney said. He didn't care about any of that. He painted because he liked solving the technical problems.

I looked carefully at the seascape. The rendering of water and sand and rocks was precise but instead of a methodical coldness there was an air of peace and wonder at the ordinary existence of things. Even when people don't know what they are feeling, it comes out in word slips and glances and strokes of paint.

'I take lots of photographs, visit the place I want to paint in different lights, but I paint at home.' Barney said. 'I can't stand for long – the pain comes back – so I don't paint outside anymore.'

'So the pain is still there. I thought it was okay now.'

'It is most of the time. They told me it would be for the rest of my life, but about a year ago it lifted. I don't know why. Now it's just when I stand up for too long, or walk too far.'

'Do you think it changed you? Dealing with pain, I mean? I think it would make me angry.'

Jenny looked at him. I could see she wanted to say something but didn't know if she should speak for him. He was still trying to find the words.

'He's more accepting,' Jenny said.

'Of what?'

'Of other people. Of help from other people. He was very self-reliant. Now he knows that we all need each other. That it's okay not to be able to do everything. To be vulnerable. And it's okay for other people not to be capable either.'

Barney nodded.

Lunch was nearly over. Jenny brought a bowl of strawberries and cherries and put them in the middle of the table.

# Chrysalis

'Cherries always remind me of Dad,' I said. 'He loved them.'

Barney looked at me and nodded again. 'Me too.' His eyes were warm with remembering our father and – I felt sure – with knowing we had the same picture in our heads. Our mother stewed the cherries and gave them to him in a bowl, sometimes with custard or ice-cream, and he ate them with such pleasure. The whole family sprang into being around our mother and father in the shabby kitchen.

Barney got up and limped away into one of the spare bedrooms. I hadn't noticed before that he limped so badly. He came out with a small painting in his hand.

'This is for you,' he said. 'It's called *Reading Glasses*.'

It was an oil painting of a glass of red wine, wire-framed reading glasses and an exact rendition of one of my books sitting on a wooden table. It was the book with a magpie on the cover, about the land we grew up on. The corners of the painted book were turned up as if it had been well read.

When I arrived back home after the trip north, I made the fact-check corrections Barney had given me. Then I emailed and thanked him for answering all my questions and for *Reading Glasses*. He sent me a track-log of his latest flight. He said the air had been choppy and his wing had collapsed at one point but he was thousands of feet up and had been able to correct it. He added that he and Jenny were coming down to Sydney in November and asked if we would be back from our latest walk. 'We'd like to come and visit,' he said.

'Yes,' I said.

It's a couple of months away and I have several hundreds of kilometres to walk before then, but I am looking forward to

# The JOY of HIGH PLACES

Barney's visit. I take a photograph of the map of where I will be walking next, from Port-La-Nouvelle to Foix in south-eastern France, and email it to him. The narrow red line scrawls across shaded mountains and rivers and appears simple until you zoom in close. It looks a lot like Barney's track-log looping above the landscape, a long script imprinted on the countryside. It looks like it could keep going forever.

# Acknowledgments

The first and deepest gratitude is owed to my brother, Barney Miller, without whom this book could not have been written. His generosity and thoroughness with my persistent questions have been extraordinary. Thank you Barney. I hope you will forgive any inaccuracies that may remain. You know I can't always be trusted with the facts, but this time I have tried.

Many thanks are due to Delia Falconer, Pamela Freeman and Anthony Reeder, who all said the right things at the right time. Their insights and suggestions kept me from getting lost for too long.

Thank you also to my agent Clare Forster for her thoughtful comments and support, and to publisher Phillipa McGuinness, editors Paul O'Beirne and Fiona Sim, cover designer Peter Long and all the team at NewSouth for their support and care.

I want to acknowledge the Anangu and Adnyamathanha people for the cultural knowledge they have so kindly shared in various public forums, online and at tourist sites. Also Rose Chown, now deceased, of the Wiradjuri people, who allowed me to tell a little of her story and of which I've used a fragment.

The ebooks read aloud after walking each day must be acknowledged. Some of them are not mentioned in the text as I have not written about all the long-distance walks I have taken, but they have been companions:

Bouvier, Nicolas, *The Way of the World*, Eland Publications Ltd ebook, 2011.
Joyce, James, *Ulysses*, Project Gutenberg ebook, 2008.
Proust, Marcel, *In Search of Lost Time*, CK Moncrieff trans, Project Gutenberg ebook, 2009.
Rushdie, Salman, *Joseph Anton: A Memoir*, Random House epub, 2012.
Sebald, WG, *The Rings of Saturn*, Vintage digital, 2013.
White, Patrick, *Voss*, Random House epub, 2012.

These books have been a much deeper part of the walking day than I have been able to convey. I also acknowledge other books that I've mentioned:

Brontë, Emily, *Wuthering Heights*, Penguin Books, Melbourne, 2013.
Gros, Frédéric, *A Philosophy of Walking*, Verso, London, 2014.
Jung, Carl, *Man and His Symbols*, Penguin, London, 1990.
Wordsworth, William, *The Complete Works of William Wordsworth*, Delphi Classics, London, 2013.

And lines from:

Auden, WH, 'Musée des Beaux Arts', *Collected Poems*, Random House, London, 1976.

# Acknowledgments

Baxter, Sarah, *A History of the World in 500 Walks*, Australian Geographic, Sydney, 2016.

I want to acknowledge the numerous online sources I consulted; in particular:

'All God's Chillun Had Wings', Kids Stories, The Moonlit Road, <www.themoonlitroad.com/all-gods-chillun-had-wings/>.

'Animals' (topic), How Stuff Works, <www.animals.howstuffworks.com>.

Ayers Rock Resort, 'Travelling to Uluru: Natural environment', (information on Anangu botany and seasons) <www.ayersrockresort.com.au/uluru-and-kata-tjuta/natural-environment>.

Cross Country magazine, <www.xcmag.com>.

Dorey, Fran, 'Australopithecus Afarensis', Australian Museum, updated 16 November 2018, <www.australianmuseum.net.au/australopithecus-afarensis>.

Encyclopaedia Britannica, <www.britannica.com>.

Helvesi, Dennis, 'David Barish, a developer of the paraglider is dead at 88', *New York Times*, 1 January 2010, <www.nytimes.com/2010/01/01/us/01barish>.

'How Walking Benefits the Brain', Science News, Science Daily, 24 April 2017, <www.sciencedaily.com/releases/2017/04/170424141340.htm>.

Kunzig, Robert, 'The Physics of ... Walking: Why humans walk like an imperfect pendulum', *Discover*, July 2001, <www.discovermagazine.com/2001/jul/featphysics>.

'Lucy's Story', Arizona State University, Institute of Human Origins, <www.iho.asu.edu/about/lucys-story>.

National Geographic, <www.nationalgeographic.com>.

NewScientist, <www.newscientist.com>.

Omniglot, <www.omniglot.com>.

Schiller Center for Connective Change, <www.schiller.org>.

Science Daily, <www.sciencedaily.com/releases/2017/04/170424141340.htm>.

Scottish Natural Heritage, <www.snh.org.uk>.

Walking Britain, <www.walkingbritain.co.uk>.

'Walking Upright', Smithsonian National Museum of Natural History, <humanorigins.si.edu/human-characteristics/walking-upright>.

*Wikipedia* for being a useful quick check of the names of birds and flowers and other important details.

Wong, May, 'Stanford Study Finds Walking Improves Creativity', Stanford News, 24 April 2014, <www.news.stanford.edu/2014/04/24/walking-vs-sitting-042414/>.

Finally I want to thank Anthony Reeder, again, not just for his editorial comments, and not just for reading me the whole of *Ulysses* – although that alone is enough – but also for his fierce engagement with the endlessly challenging process of writing.